10 Ways to Love My Wife:

WE STILL DO MARRIAGE EDITION

I0105913

APOSTLE PAUL CAMPBELL, JR.

Copyright © 2024 Paul Campbell, Jr.

All rights reserved. No part of this book may be reproduced in any form or by any electronic or mechanical means, including information storage and retrieval systems, without permission in writing from the publisher, except by reviewers, who may quote brief passages in a review.

Print ISBN: 978-1-955312-89-9

eBook ISBN: 978-1-955312-90-5

Printed in the United States of America

Story Corner Publishing & Consulting, Inc.

Chesapeake, VA 23321

Storycornerpublishing@yahoo.com

www.StoryCornerPublishing.com

Dedication

I dedicate this book to all the husbands who wanted to call it quits, who no longer wanted to stay in the good fight of marriage, and those who failed to realize or remember their true purpose in marriage.

"So they are no longer two, but one flesh. Therefore, what God has joined together, let no one separate." (Matthew 19:6)

Contents

Introduction
THE CALL TO LOVE YOUR WIFE

Growing up, I had many examples in my life of how to love a wife. Over time, however, I realized that not all examples were good ones to follow. I tried doing all the "right" things—opening doors, praying with and for her, walking on the outside of the street to protect her, and so on. But as I observed actions that didn't reflect God's love, I knew they would fail. I promised myself that when I got married, I wouldn't settle for anything less than the love God intended.

As we dive into the heart of this book, there are a few things I want to address. For the longest time, I thought I knew what love was. I thought it was what I'd seen growing up—words like "I love you," acts of kindness, gifts, money, hugs, sex, and relationships. But I was wrong. And so were the examples that taught me those ideas of "love."

I grew up in church and always knew about God. I heard about His love all the time, but I thought it was general—meant for humanity as a whole, not something specific for couples. Crazy, right? But the truth is, there are many ways to express love, yet only one true way to love: God's way.

So, what is God's love? God's love is steadfast and unchanging. It is sacrificial, pure, and unconditional. God's love is a gift. We can see His love in the blessings He gives us—from the beauty of creation to the people He places in our lives. His love is evident in both the big and small things He does for us, because He cherishes us.

Ephesians 3:18 reminds us that God's love surpasses our understanding. It is wide, long, high, and deep. Loving God is the most important commandment, and loving our neighbor flows naturally from it (Mark 12:29-31). To truly understand how to love your wife, you first need to know how to love God and learn how God loves you.

I've loved my wife for many years, and I still love her deeply. But when we first got married, my love for her wasn't necessarily the kind of love she needed. Love takes different forms in different contexts—we love our friends, family, church, and God in unique ways. However, we often use the words "I love you" without fully grasping their weight. Love isn't just a feeling or emotion, as the world often portrays it. Love is an action that others can see and experience.

Love is the act of valuing someone more than yourself—it's about sacrifice. It's about wanting others to succeed, be happy, and fulfilled. God created us to love as He loves and to be loved. Sadly, even in the church, we often fall short of fully reflecting God's love. But here's the good news: God's love never fails.

God consistently and deliberately values us more than Himself. He places us before Himself—remember, the cross is the ultimate expression of this sacrificial love. To love your wife in the way God intends, you must model your love after His. True love is selfless, enduring, and rooted in faith. It is love that not only honors your spouse but also glorifies God.

Marriage is one of God's greatest gifts and most profound relationship He created. It's a covenant designed to reflect His love for His people—a union built on love, sacrifice, and faithfulness. As a husband, God has entrusted you with the sacred responsibility of loving your wife as Christ loves the church. This isn't just about romance or grand gestures, though those are important—it's about cultivating a lifelong partnership rooted in selflessness, commitment, and faith. This is a high calling, requiring sacrifice and intentionality.

In Ephesians 5:25, Paul gives husbands a charge: *"Husbands, love your wives, just as Christ loved the church and gave himself up for her."* Think about that for a moment. Christ's love for the church is patient, sacrificial, forgiving, and unconditional. He laid down His life for her, even when she was undeserving. As a husband, you are called to model that same love for your wife—an extraordinary and humbling task.

But what does it truly mean to love your wife in a way that pleases God and brings joy to her life? It means being intentional about how you show love, honor, and care in everyday life. It means serving her with humility, leading her with wisdom, and building a relationship where she feels secure, cherished, and valued.

This book is not just a guide; it's an invitation. An invitation to grow deeper in your marriage, to align your actions with God's Word, and to pursue your wife with renewed passion and purpose. Whether you've been married for decades or are just beginning your journey, these biblical principles offer practical ways to strengthen your relationship and reflect God's design for marriage.

Through the following chapters, we will explore 10 important ways to love your wife and keep her happy, rooted in Scripture and shaped by God's perfect wisdom. From leading with love to appreciating her daily, these practices will help you build a marriage that not only thrives but also honors the Lord.

As you read, ask God to reveal areas where you can grow as a husband. Reflect on His Word, seek His guidance, and rely on His strength to become the partner your wife needs and deserves. With God at the center of your marriage, there is no limit to the joy, intimacy, and fulfillment you can experience together.

Marriage is not a destination but a journey—one where love is continually refined and deepened. As you embark on this journey, remember that your love for your wife is a reflection of God's love for you: sacrificial, enduring, and full of grace.

Let this book inspire you to love your wife wholeheartedly, build a marriage that glorifies God, and create a bond that will stand the test of time. As Proverbs 18:22 reminds us, *"He who finds a wife finds what is good and receives favor from the Lord."* Your wife is a precious gift from God, and it is because of her that you obtain favor from God. Therefore, cherish her, honor her, and love her in a way that reflects the favor you've been given from God.

Welcome to the journey of cherishing her. Let's begin.

Chapter 1
LOVE HER UNCONDITIONALLY

"Love never fails." (1 Corinthians 13:8)

There are many types of love, but unconditional love is the foundation of a godly and thriving marriage. When you vowed to love your wife, you committed to loving her not just in moments of ease and joy but also through challenges, disagreements, and trials. Unconditional love is not based on performance, mood, or circumstances—it is steadfast and unwavering, reflecting God's perfect love for us.

What is Unconditional Love?

Unconditional love mirrors the agape love that God shows to humanity. It is selfless, sacrificial, and enduring. In marriage, this love means choosing to love your wife no matter what—whether she's having a bad day, whether she disappoints you, or whether life gets hard. It's about loving her for who she is, not what she does for you.

The Bible provides the perfect definition of love in 1 Corinthians 13:4-7:

"Love is patient, love is kind. It does not envy, it does not boast, it is not proud. It does not dishonor others, it is not self-seeking, it is not easily angered, it keeps no record of wrongs. Love does not delight in evil but rejoices with the truth. It always protects, always trusts, always hopes, always perseveres."

This passage serves as a blueprint for how a husband should love his wife.

Why Unconditional Love Matters

Unconditional love provides security in your marriage. It assures your wife that your love isn't fleeting or dependent on external factors. This kind of love:

- **Reflects Christ's Love:** In Ephesians 5:25, husbands are called to love their wives as Christ loved the church. Christ's love is sacrificial and enduring, even in our imperfections.

- **Strengthens Trust:** When your wife knows she is loved unconditionally, she feels safe to be vulnerable and authentic with you.

- **Builds Resilience:** Life is full of ups and downs, but unconditional love anchors your marriage, allowing you to weather storms together.

Practical Ways to Love Her Unconditionally

1. Love Her Through Her Flaws

No one is perfect—not you, and not your wife. Loving her unconditionally means embracing her imperfections and choosing grace over criticism. Just as God's love covers our shortcomings, your love should cover hers.

Scripture: *"Above all, love each other deeply, because love covers over a multitude of sins." (1 Peter 4:8)*

Application:

- Resist the urge to point out every mistake or flaw.

- Instead of criticizing, offer encouragement and solutions.

- Acknowledge your own imperfections to create a culture of grace.

2. Be Patient and Forgiving

Unconditional love requires patience, especially during disagreements or when emotions run high. Forgiveness is also crucial—holding onto grudges or keeping score undermines the security and peace of your marriage.

Scripture: *"Bear with each other and forgive one another if any of you has a grievance against someone. Forgive as the Lord forgave you." (Colossians 3:13)*

Application:

- Pause and pray before reacting during conflicts.

- Seek to understand her perspective, even if you disagree.

- Let go of past mistakes and choose to move forward together.

3. Show Love in Action, Not Just Words

While telling your wife you love her is important, actions speak louder than words. Demonstrating love through kindness, service, and consistency shows her that your love is genuine.

Scripture: *"Let us not love with words or speech but with actions and in truth." (1 John 3:18)*

Application:

- Serve her in practical ways, like helping with chores or taking care of errands.

- Surprise her with thoughtful gestures, like a handwritten note or her favorite treat.

- Be consistent in your love, even during difficult times.

4. Love Her When She Feels Unlovable

There will be times when your wife feels insecure, overwhelmed, or distant. In these moments, she needs your love the most. Reassure her of her worth and beauty, and remind her that your love is unwavering.

Scripture: *"We love because He first loved us." (1 John 4:19)*

Application:

- Affirm her beauty, worth, and value regularly.

- Hold her when she's upset and let her know you're there for her.

- Be her safe space where she feels accepted, even in moments of doubt or struggle.

5. Prioritize Her Needs Above Your Own

Loving your wife unconditionally means putting her needs before your own. This doesn't mean neglecting yourself, but it does mean sacrificing selfish desires for the sake of your marriage and her happiness.

Scripture: *"Do nothing out of selfish ambition or vain conceit. Rather, in humility value others above yourselves." (Philippians 2:3)*

Application:

- Be attentive to her emotional, physical, and spiritual needs.

- Make decisions with her well-being in mind.

- Be willing to compromise when necessary.

Obstacles to Unconditional Love

Loving unconditionally isn't easy. There will be times when selfishness, pride, or frustration gets in the way. To overcome these obstacles:

1. **Stay Rooted in God's Word:** Regularly meditate on Scriptures that teach about love and marriage.

2. **Pray for Strength:** Ask God to help you love your wife as He loves you.

3. **Seek Accountability:** Surround yourself with godly mentors or friends who can encourage you in your role as a husband.

Reflection Questions

- Do you love your wife the way Christ loves the church?

- How can you show more grace and patience in your marriage?

- Are there areas where your love has been conditional?

Love has many lanes, and it's up to us to stay on the right road. Love can take many forms depending on the relationship and the value someone holds in your life. But in marriage, love should mean giving your all even friendship. Let's cut to the chase—who says you can't be friends with your wife?

Let me share a story. Before my wife and I got together, she had a best friend of over 20 years. When we began our relationship, they were still close friends. Nothing wrong with that, right? But when we got married, everything changed. And I mean *everything*. They're no longer friends because God said so. It hurt my wife deeply, and honestly, it probably still does at times. But not everything is meant to last forever. Everything in life has an expiration date.

At that time, my wife didn't know what to do, and truthfully, neither did I. She didn't yet realize that God was positioning me to be her best friend—even though I was already her husband. What's crazy is, when she finally realized it, I didn't. I had no idea how to step into that role for her. Growing up, I never really had best friends, so I didn't know how to be one for her or meet the standards she was used to. No, I couldn't be a woman like her previous best friend, but I *could* have been someone she could trust, count on, depend on, and rely on. I wasn't that for many years of our marriage. It's like I had—or maybe still have—a delayed reaction to certain things when it comes to her needs.

But I'm getting better.

Loving my wife means loving her the way God loves her. My love for her must be selfless, sacrificial, and unconditional. No matter what happens in our lives, my love must remain steadfast. I'll be the first to admit I haven't always loved her this way. For too long, my love was transactional—a "you do for me, I'll do for you" kind of love.

But here's the truth: the only love worth giving in marriage—or in any relationship—is the love of God. God's love is consistent, unwavering, and pure. That's the standard we should strive for. In marriage, this kind of love is not optional—it's essential.

Unconditional love is not always easy, but it is always worth it. By choosing to love your wife without conditions, you create a marriage that reflects God's heart and brings glory to Him. Remember, your love for your wife is a testimony of your faith and obedience to God.

"And over all these virtues put on love, which binds them all together in perfect unity." (Colossians 3:14)

Chapter 2

LISTEN ATTENTIVELY

"Everyone should be quick to listen, slow to speak and slow to become angry." (James 1:19)

Listening attentively is one of the most profound ways to express love to your wife. It is through listening that you understand her heart, her concerns, and her needs. Many marriages struggle because spouses feel unheard or dismissed, but when you commit to listening well, you create a deeper connection and foster emotional intimacy. Listening attentively is an act of selflessness that shows your wife that her voice matters and her feelings are valued.

The Importance of Listening in Marriage

1. **Builds Trust:** When you listen without interrupting or judging, your wife feels safe to share her thoughts, knowing you respect her perspective.

2. **Strengthens Emotional Connection:** Genuine listening allows you to understand her joys, struggles, and dreams, drawing you closer as a couple.

3. **Reflects God's Love:** Just as God hears our prayers with compassion, attentive listening mirrors His love and care for us.

What Does It Mean to Listen Attentively?

Listening attentively goes beyond simply hearing your wife's words. It involves:

- **Giving Undivided Attention:** Putting aside distractions like phones or TV to focus entirely on her.

- **Understanding Her Emotions:** Paying attention to not just her words but also her tone, expressions, and body language.

    o **Vali**dating Her Feelings: Acknowledging her emotions, even if you don't fully agree with her perspective.

Scripture Insight:

"The purposes of a person's heart are deep waters, but one who has insight draws them out." (Proverbs 20:5)

When you listen with care, you help your wife feel understood and appreciated, drawing out the depths of her heart.

Practical Steps to Listen Attentively

1. Be Fully Present

It's easy to get distracted by work, technology, or other responsibilities, but when your wife is speaking, she deserves your full attention. Show her that she is your priority in that moment.

Application:

- Put your phone on silent and turn off the TV during important conversations.

- Maintain eye contact to show that you're engaged.

- Lean in and use positive body language, like nodding or smiling, to encourage her to keep sharing.

2. Avoid Interrupting or Offering Quick Solutions

Sometimes, your wife may just need to vent or share her feelings without you trying to "fix" the problem. Interrupting or jumping to solutions can make her feel dismissed or unheard.

Application:

- Let her finish speaking before responding.

- Use phrases like "Tell me more" or "I'm listening" to encourage her to express herself fully.

- If she seems upset, ask, "Do you want me to listen or help you find a solution?"

Scripture: *"To answer before listening—that is folly and shame."* *(Proverbs 18:13)*

3. Listen with Empathy

Empathy means putting yourself in her shoes and understanding her feelings from her perspective. Even if you don't share her view, acknowledging her emotions can strengthen your bond.

Application:

- Reflect back what you hear: "It sounds like you're feeling frustrated because…"

- Avoid dismissing her feelings with phrases like "You're overreacting" or "It's not a big deal."

- Show compassion, even if you don't agree, by saying, "I can see why you feel that way."

4. Ask Thoughtful Questions

Good listening involves asking questions that help you understand her better. Thoughtful questions show her that you care about her thoughts and experiences.

Application:

- Ask open-ended questions like, "What's been on your mind lately?" or "How did that make you feel?"

- Avoid yes/no questions, as they can limit deeper conversation.

- Be patient if she needs time to articulate her thoughts.

Scripture: *"The wise in heart are called discerning, and gracious words promote instruction."* *(Proverbs 16:21)*

5. Be Patient and Nonjudgmental

Sometimes, your wife may share things that are difficult for you to hear or process. Listening attentively means setting aside judgment and giving her the freedom to express herself without fear of criticism.

Application:

- Stay calm and avoid defensive reactions.

- If you feel tempted to argue, take a deep breath and remind yourself that listening is about understanding, not debating.

- Pray for wisdom to respond with love and grace.

Barriers to Effective Listening

Listening attentively takes practice, and there are common obstacles that can get in the way:

1. **Distractions:** Work, phones, or other interruptions can pull your focus away.

2. **Prejudgments:** Assuming you already know what she's going to say can hinder genuine listening.

3. **Defensiveness:** Feeling attacked or criticized can make you more focused on responding than understanding.

How to Overcome Barriers:

- Schedule uninterrupted time to talk when both of you are free from distractions.

- Pray for humility and an open heart before important conversations.

- Practice active listening by summarizing what she says before sharing your thoughts.

Scriptural Inspiration for Listening

The Bible emphasizes the value of listening throughout Scripture.

o   *"My* dear brothers and sisters, take note of this: Everyone should be quick to listen, slow to speak and slow to become angry." (James 1:*19)*

This verse reminds us that listening is a priority in any relationship, especially in marriage.

o   *"The heart of the* discerning acquires knowledge, for the ears of the wise seek it out." *(Proverbs 18:15)*

Listening attentively is a mark of wisdom and humility, qualities that reflect God's character.

Practical Reflection Questions

- Do I give my wife my full attention when she's speaking?

- How can I respond with empathy, even when I don't fully agree with her?

- Are there distractions or habits I need to eliminate to become a better listener?

Marriage is a lot of work, but it can also be one of the most rewarding experiences in life. A healthy, thriving marriage requires commitment and consistent, intentional habits. To keep your relationship strong, both partners have needs that should be met every single day.

As a husband, meeting your wife's needs can sometimes feel challenging—especially when you feel like your own needs aren't being met. It's easy to fall into the mindset of, *"Why should I meet her needs if mine aren't being fulfilled?"* But the truth is, loving your wife the way God calls you to requires selflessness. In those moments, you must put her needs above your own.

If you're unsure of what your wife needs from you, don't let pride keep you from asking. Simply ask her, and she will tell you. Understanding her needs opens the door to deeper connection and greater intimacy.

Husbands, even when you don't feel like saying "I love you," remember the power in those three words. Say it anyway and watch how your wife reacts. You'll likely find that it not only brings her joy but also makes you feel closer to her.

Another way to nurture your marriage is by showing gratitude. Turn your focus outward and reflect on all the good things your wife does and the reasons why you love her. Acknowledging her efforts and qualities will deepen your love for her and fill her heart with happiness. Gratitude is a simple yet profound way to express love, and it strengthens the bond between you.

Marriage thrives when selflessness, love, and gratitude become daily practices. By committing to these, you'll not only meet your wife's needs but also create a relationship that honors God and brings joy to both of you.

Listening attentively is one of the simplest yet most powerful ways to love your wife. It communicates respect, value, and care, deepening your connection and building trust in your marriage. By prioritizing her voice and learning to truly understand her heart, you fulfill your God-given role as her partner and protector.

Listening isn't just a skill—it's a form of love that mirrors the attentive care of God. As Psalm 34:15 reminds us, *"The eyes of the Lord are on the righteous, and his ears are attentive to their cry."* Just as God listens to us, may we learn to listen to our wives with the same care and compassion.

Chapter 3

LEAD WITH LOVE

"Husbands, love your wives, just as Christ loved the church and gave himself up for her." (Ephesians 5:25)

L eadership in marriage is not about dominance or control; it is about loving stewardship. As a husband, God has called you to be the spiritual leader of your home, a responsibility that requires humility, wisdom, and love. Leading with love means modeling Christ's sacrificial and selfless love, putting your wife's well-being and spiritual growth at the forefront of your actions.

True leadership in marriage is rooted in service and devotion, creating an environment where your wife feels cherished, protected, and valued. It is not about asserting authority but about taking the initiative to nurture your marriage and honor God in your relationship.

What Does It Mean to Lead with Love?

Leadership in marriage isn't about making all the decisions or demanding submission. It is about guiding your marriage toward Christ, supporting your wife's needs, and ensuring that both of you grow closer to God and to each other. Leading with love means:

1. **Sacrificing for Your Wife:** Just as Christ sacrificed for the church, you are called to prioritize her needs above your own.

2. **Encouraging Her Growth:** This includes spiritual, emotional, and personal growth, helping her become all that God has called her to be.

3. **Setting a Godly Example:** Your actions, words, and decisions should reflect Christ's love and wisdom.

Why Leading with Love Matters

1. **Reflects Christ in Your Marriage:** Your leadership should mirror how Christ loves and leads His people—with patience, grace, and compassion.

2. **Fosters a Safe Environment:** When you lead with love, your wife feels secure, respected, and valued, which strengthens trust and intimacy.

3. **Builds a Strong Foundation:** Loving leadership sets the tone for a marriage that thrives spiritually, emotionally, and physically.

Practical Ways to Lead with Love

1. Be a Servant Leader

Christ's leadership was marked by humility and service. He washed His disciples' feet and ultimately laid down His life for them. As a husband, your leadership should reflect this servant-hearted approach.

Scripture:

"The greatest among you will be your servant." (Matthew 23:11)

Application:

- Serve your wife in practical ways, such as helping with household tasks or taking care of responsibilities she may find overwhelming.

- Ask her how you can support her and be attentive to her needs.

- Lead by example, showing humility and a willingness to serve.

2. Make Decisions with Her Best Interest in Mind

Leadership in marriage often involves making decisions, but this doesn't mean making them alone or based solely on your preferences. Leading with love requires considering your wife's input, feelings, and needs.

Scripture:

"Do nothing out of selfish ambition or vain conceit. Rather, in humility value others above yourselves." (Philippians 2:3)

Application:

- Include your wife in decisions, and genuinely consider her perspective.

- Pray together before making significant choices, seeking God's guidance as a team.

- Be willing to compromise when needed for the greater good of your marriage.

3. Lead Spiritually

As the spiritual leader of your home, you are responsible for nurturing a Christ-centered marriage. This involves prioritizing prayer, Bible study, and worship, both individually and as a couple.

Scripture:

"But as for me and my household, we will serve the Lord." (Joshua 24:15)

Application:

- Establish regular times for prayer and devotionals with your wife.

- Encourage her spiritual growth by supporting her involvement in church, Bible studies, or ministry.

- Live out your faith in everyday life, setting a godly example through your words and actions.

4. Communicate with Love and Clarity

Effective leadership requires clear and loving communication. Your tone, words, and approach should always reflect care and respect.

Scripture:

"Let your conversation be always full of grace, seasoned with salt, so that you may know how to answer everyone." (Colossians 4:6)

Application:

- Speak with kindness and avoid harsh or dismissive language.

- Be transparent about your thoughts and decisions, inviting her input.

- Address conflicts with patience and a desire to find resolution together.

5. Be Willing to Sacrifice

Loving leadership often requires sacrificing your own desires, time, or comfort for the sake of your wife. This mirrors Christ's love for the church, where He gave everything for her.

Scripture:

"Greater love has no one than this: to lay down one's life for one's friends." (John 15:13)

Application:

- Prioritize your wife's needs above your own, especially during challenging times.

- Sacrifice time for hobbies or work to spend quality time with her.

- Be attentive to her emotional and physical well-being, even if it means adjusting your plans.

Challenges to Leading with Love

Leadership is not always easy, and there are challenges that may arise, such as:

1. **Pride:** The temptation to prioritize your own desires or assert authority over your wife.

2. **Passivity:** Avoiding leadership responsibilities out of fear or uncertainty.

3. **Frustration:** Reacting impatiently or harshly during conflicts or stressful situations.

How to Overcome Challenges:

- Pray for humility and wisdom to lead with a Christ-like heart.

- Seek guidance from God's Word and mentors who can support you in your role as a husband.

- Apologize and seek forgiveness when you fall short, demonstrating accountability.

Scriptural Inspiration for Leading with Love

- "Do everything in love." (1 Corinthians 16:14)

- This verse reminds us that love should be the driving force behind every action and decision in marriage.

- "Above all, love each other deeply, because love covers over a multitude of sins." (1 Peter 4:8)

Deep love fosters grace and forgiveness, essential qualities for a husband who leads with love.

Reflection Questions

- Do I lead my marriage with love, humility, and selflessness?

- How can I better serve and support my wife's needs?

- Are there areas where I need to grow as a spiritual leader in my home?

Your wife needs to feel valued and respected in your marriage. When faced with a difficult decision, it's important to talk it through with her first. Remember, the two of you are now one, and every decision you make affects her life as well. Work together toward common goals and approach challenges as a team.

If you and your wife have conflicting opinions, take the time to listen to each other. Give her the opportunity to share her thoughts, just as you share yours, and work together to reach a compromise. Viewing your wife as an equal partner—not an assistant—is essential. When you treat her as anything less, it will show in your actions and can lead to frustration and division in your marriage.

Respect in marriage is vital. What you sow into your relationship will grow—whether it's respect and love or neglect and chaos. I've learned this lesson the hard way. For years, I didn't respect my wife for who she is or acknowledge all she has done. I didn't see her as my equal in any way. Instead, I behaved as if I were the only one in the marriage, disregarding her thoughts, feelings, and contributions.

At the start of our marriage, I even took counsel from people who painted a negative picture of my wife and our relationship. Unfortunately, I believed them. Their words influenced me to dishonor and disrespect my wife—not only through my actions but sometimes through my lack of action. This created unnecessary tension and scars in our relationship.

But everything changed when God opened my eyes. He gave me a revelation of how He designed marriage to reflect His love. I realized the damage I'd caused, and though I'm still a work in progress, I'm committed to treating my wife with the honor and respect she deserves.

Husbands, don't make the same mistakes I did. The harm caused by disrespect can leave lasting wounds on your wife's heart and create needless struggles in your marriage. Instead, value her as your equal partner and cherish her as God intended. Treat your wife with respect and honor—always.

Leading with love is not about authority but about serving your wife with the same sacrificial love that Christ showed the church. It is a call to selflessness, patience, and devotion, creating a marriage that honors God and fulfills your wife's deepest needs.

When you lead with love, you reflect Christ's heart and build a foundation for a marriage that thrives in every season. Remember, your role as a loving leader is a God-given responsibility—one that requires daily reliance on His wisdom, strength, and grace.

"Be completely humble and gentle; be patient, bearing with one another in love." (Ephesians 4:2)

Chapter 4

THE IMPORTANCE OF HONESTY AND LOYALTY IN MARRIAGE

"Therefore each of you must put off falsehood and speak truthfully to your neighbor, for we are all members of one body."
(Ephesians 4:25)

Honesty and loyalty are two foundational pillars that uphold a marriage, ensuring trust, intimacy, and long-lasting love. Without these virtues, a marriage can become strained, leaving room for misunderstandings, resentment, and brokenness. Honesty and loyalty, grounded in God's Word, not only protect the marriage relationship but also reflect the integrity and faithfulness of God Himself.

Marriage is designed to be a covenant of truth and fidelity, where both partners stand together, united in love and trust. Just as God is faithful and truthful to His promises, so are we called to embody these qualities in our relationships. In this chapter, we will explore why honesty and loyalty are so vital to the health and strength of a marriage, and how Scripture calls us to embody these traits in our relationship with our spouse.

Why Honesty and Loyalty Matter in Marriage

1. Honesty Builds Trust

Trust is the bedrock of any successful marriage. Without trust, the relationship falters. Honesty cultivates trust, as it enables both spouses to be transparent and open with each other. When both partners speak the truth, even when it's difficult, they demonstrate respect and care for each other. Truthfulness fosters a sense of security and intimacy, allowing the couple to grow together in love.

Scripture:

"An honest witness does not deceive, but a false witness pours out lies." (Proverbs 14:5)

When both partners commit to honesty, the marriage is built on a foundation that can withstand the challenges of life. Lies and deception erode trust and cause emotional pain, but truth strengthens the bond between husband and wife, allowing for deep emotional connection and mutual understanding.

2. **Loyalty Protects the Marriage**

Loyalty in marriage means being committed to your spouse through both the good and the bad. It means prioritizing the marriage above all other relationships and external distractions. Loyalty fosters an unbreakable bond of commitment and makes the marriage resistant to outside pressures. When loyalty is present, spouses are able to face challenges together, knowing they are on the same team, working toward shared goals and values.

Scripture:

"So they are no longer two, but one flesh. Therefore what God has joined together, let no one separate." (Matthew 19:6)

Loyalty reflects God's design for marriage as a covenant that should not be broken. Just as Christ is loyal to the Church, a husband and wife are called to be loyal to each other, no matter the circumstances. Loyalty ensures that both spouses remain committed, even when life becomes difficult or when temptation arises.

The Role of Honesty in a Marriage

1. **Honesty in Communication:**

Effective communication is the heart of a healthy marriage, and honesty is its cornerstone. This means being truthful about your feelings, your needs, and your desires. It involves being vulnerable enough to share your deepest thoughts and also being open to hearing your spouse's perspective without judgment. Honesty in communication ensures that misunderstandings are addressed and that both partners feel heard and valued.

Scripture:

"Let your conversation be always full of grace, seasoned with salt, so that you may know how to answer everyone." (Colossians 4:6)

Honest communication promotes a deep emotional connection between spouses. When you speak truthfully and respectfully, you create a space where both partners can be authentic, leading to greater understanding and intimacy.

2. **Honesty in Difficult Conversations:**

Difficult conversations are inevitable in any marriage. Whether it's discussing finances, parenting, or disagreements, being honest and transparent is crucial. Avoiding difficult conversations or hiding the truth only leads to resentment and division. When you are willing to have honest and open discussions—even about uncomfortable topics—you build a relationship founded on trust and mutual respect.

Scripture:

"Better is open rebuke than hidden love. Wounds from a friend can be trusted, but an enemy multiplies kisses." (Proverbs 27:5-6)

Honesty may at times bring temporary discomfort, but it ultimately strengthens the marriage. By addressing issues head-on and being truthful, you show your commitment to the health and longevity of the relationship. This openness allows for healing and growth.

The Role of Loyalty in a Marriage

1. **Loyalty in Actions:**

Loyalty is not just a word but an action. It is demonstrated in the way you treat your spouse, the choices you make, and the time you invest in the relationship. Being loyal means prioritizing your spouse above all others and honoring the covenant you made. In the same way, Christ demonstrated His loyalty to the Church through His sacrificial love, husbands and wives are called to demonstrate their loyalty through selflessness and commitment.

Scripture:

"Let love and faithfulness never leave you; bind them around your neck, write them on the tablet of your heart." (Proverbs 3:3)

Loyalty is reflected in the little things—the acts of kindness, the gestures of affection, and the consistent devotion to your spouse. By remaining loyal, you ensure that the marriage remains a source of joy and stability.

2. **Loyalty in Times of Trial:**

Every marriage faces trials, whether due to personal struggles, financial difficulties, or external pressures. Loyalty in marriage means standing by your spouse through these challenges, supporting them with your love and prayers. It means choosing your spouse every day, even when circumstances are hard. Loyalty is what keeps couples together when life's storms arise, and it allows the marriage to thrive through adversity.

Scripture:

"Two are better than one, because they have a good return for their labor: If either of them falls down, one can help the other up." (Ecclesiastes 4:9-10)

Loyalty ensures that even when things are difficult, the bond between husband and wife remains unshaken. Loyalty is a constant reminder that no matter the challenges, you will face them together, as partners committed to each other.

Practical Ways to Cultivate Honesty and Loyalty

1. **Commit to Transparency:**

Be open and honest in your conversations. Share your thoughts, feelings, and concerns with your spouse in a respectful and loving manner. Avoid hiding things from your spouse, as secrecy undermines trust and intimacy.

2. Support Each Other Unconditionally:

Be loyal in both words and actions. Show your spouse that you will stand by them no matter what. Offer emotional support, be their confidant, and reassure them of your unwavering commitment.

3. Pray Together for Strength:

Pray for honesty and loyalty in your marriage. Ask God to help you remain truthful in all areas of your life and to give you the strength to be loyal and faithful to each other. Prayer invites God's presence into your marriage and strengthens the bond between you.

Scripture:

"And if one can overpower him who is alone, two can resist him. A cord of three strands is not quickly torn apart." (Ecclesiastes 4:12)

By inviting God into your marriage, you allow Him to guide you in maintaining honesty and loyalty. With God's help, your marriage will stand firm, even in the face of adversity.

Reflection Questions:

- Are there areas in my marriage where I have not been completely honest with my spouse?

- How can I demonstrate greater loyalty to my spouse, especially during challenging times?

- How can I improve communication and trust in my marriage through greater transparency?

Honesty and loyalty are not just ideals—they are essential qualities for a strong, lasting marriage. By embracing the truth and remaining loyal to your spouse, you create an environment where love can thrive. These virtues not only strengthen the relationship but also reflect the faithfulness and integrity of God Himself. Through honesty and loyalty, you build a marriage that honors God and stands as a testimony of His love and grace. Let your marriage be marked by truthfulness, commitment, and a deep, unwavering loyalty that mirrors the covenant God has made with His people.

Chapter 5

THE DANGER OF PRIDE, COMPETITION, AND JEALOUSY IN MARRIAGE

"Pride goes before destruction, a haughty spirit before a fall."
(Proverbs 16:18)

Pride, competition, and jealousy are three dangerous forces that can silently erode the foundation of a marriage. These destructive attitudes create division, foster insecurity, and undermine the deep love that should exist between a husband and wife. As believers in Christ, we are called to put aside pride, relinquish unhealthy competition, and overcome jealousy by allowing God to cultivate humility, love, and unity in our marriages. This chapter explores how pride, competition, and jealousy can harm a marriage and how Scripture guides us toward humility, cooperation, and contentment in the relationship.

Why Pride, Competition, and Jealousy Are Harmful to Marriage

1. Pride Breeds Division and Insecurity

Pride is rooted in self-centeredness. It leads us to prioritize our own desires, needs, and ego over the well-being of our spouse and the health of the marriage. When pride enters the relationship, it creates distance between partners, as each one seeks to assert their own importance rather than lift up the other. Pride prevents us from acknowledging our faults, making it difficult to reconcile when conflicts arise. A prideful heart is unwilling to apologize or admit weaknesses, which can drive a wedge in the relationship.

Scripture:

"Do nothing out of selfish ambition or vain conceit. Rather, in humility value others above yourselves, not looking to your own

interests but each of you to the interests of the others. " (Philippians 2:3-4)

In marriage, we are called to value our spouse above ourselves, to seek their interests and well-being, rather than being driven by our own pride. Humility is the antidote to pride, and humility fosters a relationship where both partners can thrive, forgive, and grow together in love.

2. Competition Undermines Unity

Marriage is not a rivalry but a partnership. The idea of competition in marriage, whether it's over finances, success, or recognition, undermines the unity that should exist between husband and wife. Rather than working together toward shared goals, competition creates an environment where each partner vies for personal victory, often at the expense of the other. A competitive spirit breeds resentment, making it difficult to support one another or celebrate each other's achievements.

Scripture:

"Two are better than one, because they have a good return for their labor: If either of them falls down, one can help the other up." (Ecclesiastes 4:9-10)

The goal of marriage is to work together as a team, building each other up, and achieving success as a unit. The Bible reminds us that unity and collaboration are far more valuable than personal accolades. When we drop the competitive mindset and focus on being partners, we create a foundation of trust and mutual respect.

3. Jealousy Destroys Trust and Contentment

Jealousy stems from insecurity and comparison. When we are jealous of our spouse, it reflects a lack of trust in them and in God's plan for our lives. Jealousy leads us to compare our spouse to others, which fosters discontentment and resentment. Instead of appreciating and loving our spouse for who they are, we become fixated on their shortcomings or perceived failures, and we begin to distrust their intentions. Jealousy not only affects our relationship with our spouse but also our relationship with God, as it questions His goodness and provision.

Scripture:

"For where you have envy and selfish ambition, there you find disorder and every evil practice." (James 3:16)

Jealousy brings disorder into a marriage and disrupts peace and harmony. It feeds a toxic cycle of insecurity and mistrust. To break free from jealousy, we must learn to be content in who God has made us and trust that He has a good plan for both our lives and the life of our marriage.

The Biblical Remedy: Humility, Cooperation, and Contentment

1. Embrace Humility

Humility is the opposite of pride, and it is the key to a thriving, God-honoring marriage. When we embrace humility, we acknowledge that our spouse has unique qualities and strengths that complement our own. Humility teaches us to value our spouse's perspective, to listen more than we speak, and to recognize that we do not have all the answers. It also enables us to serve our spouse with a loving heart, putting their needs before our own.

Scripture:

"Humble yourselves before the Lord, and He will lift you up." (James 4:10)

Humility invites God into our marriages to bring healing, growth, and restoration. As we humble ourselves before Him and serve our spouse with a spirit of grace and love, God honors our efforts and strengthens the bond between us.

2. Promote Cooperation Over Competition

Marriage is about teamwork, not competition. When we work together, we can accomplish far more than if we are trying to "win" individually. God created marriage as a union, a covenant where two become one, not just physically, but emotionally and spiritually. A cooperative mindset fosters love, trust, and mutual support. It encourages spouses to celebrate one another's successes and to lift each other up when facing challenges. In marriage, there should be no "I" but only "we."

Scripture:

"Let nothing be done through strife or vainglory; but in lowliness of mind let each esteem other better than themselves." (Philippians 2:3)

When we stop competing with our spouse and start cooperating, we demonstrate love, trust, and a commitment to the unity of the marriage. In every area of life, from raising children to managing finances, cooperation ensures that both spouses are working toward the same goal.

3. Cultivate Contentment

Jealousy stems from discontentment, so the remedy is learning to be content with what God has given us. Instead of comparing our spouse to others, we should focus on their unique gifts, talents, and the things we love most about them. Contentment comes when we trust God's plan for our marriage and our lives, knowing that He has already blessed us abundantly.

Scripture:

"But godliness with contentment is great gain." (1 Timothy 6:6)

When we choose contentment, we eliminate jealousy and focus on the blessings God has given us in our marriage. We stop comparing and start appreciating. Contentment in marriage leads to peace, joy, and greater satisfaction, as we celebrate what God has already provided rather than longing for what we don't have.

Practical Ways to Overcome Pride, Competition, and Jealousy

1. Examine Your Heart:

Regularly check your heart for signs of pride, competition, or jealousy. Ask yourself if you're putting your spouse's needs before your own or if you're motivated by selfish desires. Acknowledge these feelings and surrender them to God, asking for His help in cultivating humility, love, and contentment.

2. **Celebrate Your Spouse's Successes:**

Instead of feeling competitive or jealous, celebrate your spouse's victories, big and small. Be their biggest cheerleader, and express gratitude for their accomplishments. This fosters a spirit of unity and shows your spouse that you value them.

3. **Practice Gratitude:**

Make a habit of thanking God for your spouse and the unique qualities they bring to the marriage. Recognize the gifts, talents, and character of your spouse, and focus on what they offer to the relationship rather than comparing them to others. Gratitude helps us cultivate a heart of contentment.

4. **Pray for Unity:**

Pray regularly for unity in your marriage. Ask God to remove any seeds of pride, competition, or jealousy, and replace them with humility, cooperation, and love. Pray that both you and your spouse would grow together spiritually and emotionally, working as a team to fulfill God's purposes for your marriage.

Reflection Questions:

- Are there areas in my marriage where pride is causing division or hurt?

- How can I work together with my spouse rather than compete against them?

- Do I find myself comparing my spouse to others, and how can I overcome jealousy?

Pride, competition, and jealousy have the potential to tear apart a marriage, but by embracing humility, cooperation, and contentment, we create an environment of love, trust, and unity. Through the strength of God's Word, we can reject these destructive forces and replace them with the virtues that honor God and strengthen our relationship. When we choose to humble ourselves, celebrate our spouse's success, and find contentment in our marriage, we reflect God's love and grace in a powerful way. Let us strive to build marriages grounded in humility, free from pride and jealousy, and focused on cooperation and unity, for in doing so, we glorify God and create a lasting, fulfilling partnership.

Chapter 6

BE HER PARTNER IN PARENTING

"Fathers, do not provoke your children to anger, but bring them up in the discipline and instruction of the Lord." (Ephesians 6:4)

Parenting is one of the most rewarding and challenging aspects of marriage. As a husband, your role in parenting is not secondary or optional but is central to the emotional, spiritual, and practical success of your family. Being a true partner in parenting means sharing the responsibilities, offering support, and working together to raise your children in a loving, nurturing, and Christ-centered environment.

Your wife needs you not only as a husband but as a co-parent who is equally invested in the well-being and development of your children. By standing side by side in this journey, you will strengthen your marriage, deepen your bond with your children, and honor God's design for family life.

The Importance of Being a Partner in Parenting

1. **Shared Responsibility:** Parenting is a joint effort that requires mutual support. When you work together, the burdens of parenting are lighter, and the joys are more meaningful.

2. **Setting a Unified Example:** Children thrive in an environment where both parents are aligned in their approach to discipline, values, and expectations.

3. **Encouraging Emotional Support:** Your wife needs your emotional partnership as she navigates the demands of parenting. By being present, you validate her efforts and provide her with the encouragement she needs.

What Does It Mean to Be a Partner in Parenting?

Being a partner in parenting means more than just helping with chores or occasionally spending time with the children. It involves a deep commitment to your role as a father and a collaborator with your wife in nurturing your children's hearts, minds, and spirits. Here are key ways you can be an active and loving partner:

1. **Active Involvement:** Don't leave parenting to your wife alone. Take an active role in your children's lives—help with daily routines, participate in their education, and engage in their emotional development.

2. **Consistent Discipline:** Work with your wife to set consistent expectations and discipline strategies that both of you can uphold.

3. **Shared Decision Making:** Major parenting decisions—like schooling, health care, and spiritual education—should be made together, with both of your perspectives and concerns in mind.

4. **Spiritual Leadership:** Lead together in guiding your children toward faith. Pray together, teach biblical values, and ensure that your home is a place where faith is nurtured and practiced.

Practical Ways to Be Her Partner in Parenting

1. Communicate Openly About Parenting Goals

A key aspect of being a partner in parenting is having open conversations with your wife about your shared goals and approaches. This is especially important for difficult or complex issues such as discipline, education, and faith training.

Scripture:

"Iron sharpens iron, and one man sharpens another." (Proverbs 27:17)

Application:

- Take time regularly to discuss parenting, share your concerns, and offer solutions.

- Listen to your wife's thoughts and be open to compromise and growth in your parenting style.

- Set clear goals as parents and work together to achieve them.

2. Share Household Responsibilities Equally

Parenting extends beyond caring for the children—it also includes maintaining the home. By sharing the household duties equally, you create a balanced partnership that fosters peace and cooperation.

Scripture:

"Each of you should look not only to your own interests, but also to the interests of others." (Philippians 2:4)

Application:

- Help with household chores like cooking, cleaning, and organizing.

- Offer to take care of the children during stressful times or when your wife needs a break.

- Recognize when your wife is overwhelmed and step in to lighten her load.

3. Be an Active Participant in Your Children's Lives

From school activities to hobbies, being an involved father shows your children that they matter to you. This not only strengthens your relationship with them but also supports your wife in managing the daily responsibilities of raising children.

Scripture:

"Fathers, do not provoke your children to anger, but bring them up in the discipline and instruction of the Lord." (Ephesians 6:4)

Application:

- Attend parent-teacher conferences, school events, and extracurricular activities.

- Spend one-on-one time with each child to foster strong relationships.

- Be involved in the everyday details of your children's lives, from helping with homework to talking about their day.

4. Co-Create a Vision for Family Life

Parents who work together toward a common vision for their family help create a stable, loving environment where their children feel secure. Discuss your hopes for your children's future, spiritual growth, and values, and then set a plan to live out these aspirations.

Scripture:

"Where there is no vision, the people perish." (Proverbs 29:18, KJV)

Application:

- Have regular discussions about your values, goals, and parenting vision.

- Be intentional about modeling what you want your children to learn, whether it's love, patience, or faith.

- Reinforce the importance of your family values through your actions and decisions.

5. Offer Emotional and Physical Support to Your Wife

Parenting can be emotionally and physically exhausting. Your wife needs your emotional support as much as she needs your help with parenting tasks. Offer encouragement, affirm her efforts, and help her recharge when she feels drained.

Scripture:

"Two are better than one because they have a good return for their labor: If either of them falls down, one can help the other up." (Ecclesiastes 4:9-10)

Application:

- Praise your wife for her efforts and let her know you see her hard work.

- Offer to take on tasks to give her a break when she's feeling overwhelmed.

- Spend quality time together as a couple to reconnect and recharge.

Challenges to Being a Partner in Parenting

1. **Differing Parenting Styles:** You may not always agree on how to discipline or guide your children. The key is to communicate and find a unified approach that works for both of you.

2. **Time and Energy Demands:** Parenting is exhausting, and balancing work, home, and family responsibilities can feel overwhelming at times.

3. **Lack of Support or Appreciation:** If one parent feels unsupported or unappreciated, it can lead to resentment. Be intentional about showing gratitude and support for each other's efforts.

How to Overcome These Challenges:

- Regularly check in with your wife to ensure both of you feel supported.

- Take time to reflect on your shared goals and reaffirm your commitment to them.

- Be patient and understanding when conflicts arise—working through challenges as a team strengthens your partnership.

Scriptural Inspiration for Being a Partner in Parenting

- *"Train up a child in the way he should go; even when he is old he will not depart from it." (Proverbs 22:6)*

This verse reminds us of the importance of consistent, godly guidance in raising children. As a partner in parenting, you are called to train and nurture your children together with your wife.

- *"Love your wife, as Christ loved the church and gave himself up for her." (Ephesians 5:25)*

As a husband, loving your wife sacrificially and supporting her in her parenting role is a reflection of Christ's love for the church.

Reflection Questions

- How can I become more involved in my children's daily routines and activities?

- What are some ways I can support my wife emotionally and practically in her role as a mother?

- How can we improve our communication and decision-making as a parenting team?

Being a partner in parenting means being present, engaged, and supportive in all aspects of raising your children. It's about sharing the joys and the challenges, aligning your efforts with your wife's, and leading your family together toward spiritual growth.

As you fulfill your role as a partner in parenting, remember that it is a partnership rooted in love, mutual respect, and shared responsibility. By standing together in this sacred work of raising children, you not only strengthen your marriage but also lay a firm foundation for your children's future.

Bonus: Share Responsibilities

The Power of Partnership

Marriage is a partnership that thrives on teamwork. Sharing responsibilities is not just about dividing chores or tasks—it's about building a life together where both partners feel supported and valued. When responsibilities are shared equitably, it strengthens the relationship, reduces stress, and fosters mutual respect. . Husbands always remember that your wife is your partner, not your enemy. You will either win together or lose together. The goal is to win.

This chapter explores why sharing responsibilities is essential, practical strategies to implement it in your marriage, and how it contributes to a more harmonious and fulfilling relationship.

Why Sharing Responsibilities Matters

In many marriages, uneven distribution of responsibilities can lead to frustration, resentment, and burnout. By sharing the load, you demonstrate care and commitment to each other's well-being, ensuring that neither partner feels overburdened or unappreciated.

Benefits of Sharing Responsibilities:

- Reduces stress and prevents burnout for both partners.

- Encourages teamwork and mutual respect.

- Creates a sense of fairness and balance.

- Builds a stronger emotional connection.

- Provides more time for quality moments together.

When both partners actively contribute, they create a foundation of trust and partnership, reinforcing the idea that they are in this together.

Types of Responsibilities in Marriage

1. Household Chores

Daily tasks like cooking, cleaning, grocery shopping, and laundry are necessary for maintaining a home. Sharing these duties ensures that neither partner feels overwhelmed.

2. Financial Responsibilities

Managing household finances, budgeting, paying bills, and planning for the future are crucial aspects of a shared life.

3. Emotional Support

Providing encouragement, listening to each other, and being present emotionally are responsibilities that strengthen your bond.

4. Parenting (If Applicable)

Raising children requires teamwork, from decision-making to day-to-day caregiving.

5. Relationship Maintenance

Investing time and effort into nurturing your marriage is also a shared responsibility.

Strategies for Sharing Responsibilities

1. Communicate Expectations Clearly

Openly discuss what each of you expects when it comes to responsibilities. Misaligned assumptions can lead to misunderstandings.

- **Have a Discussion:** Talk about what tasks need to be done and who will handle them.

- **Be Specific:** Instead of saying, "You handle the bills," agree on specific actions like, "You'll pay the utilities, and I'll handle the mortgage."

2. Play to Each Other's Strengths

Assign tasks based on who is better suited for them or enjoys them more.

- **Leverage Skills:** If one of you is better with numbers, they could manage the budget, while the other handles organizing household activities.

- **Rotate Tasks:** For chores neither of you enjoys, take turns to share the load equally.

3. Be Flexible and Willing to Adjust

Life circumstances change, and so should the division of responsibilities. Be open to re-evaluating and adjusting your roles as needed.

- **Check In Regularly:** Schedule periodic discussions to ensure both partners feel the workload is fair.

- **Adapt to Changes:** For example, if one partner's job becomes more demanding, the other can take on additional responsibilities temporarily.

4. Make It a Team Effort

Approach responsibilities with a team mindset rather than dividing tasks rigidly.

- **Work Together:** Cook dinner as a team or tackle cleaning the house together to make tasks feel less burdensome.

- **Share Big Decisions:** Collaborate on major life choices like budgeting, investments, or parenting strategies.

5. Use Tools to Stay Organized

Keeping track of responsibilities helps avoid misunderstandings.

- **Create a Shared Calendar:** Use a digital or physical calendar to plan chores, appointments, and activities.

- **Make Lists:** A shared to-do list can clarify what needs to be done and who is responsible.

Challenges in Sharing Responsibilities and How to Overcome Them

1. Uneven Workloads

If one partner feels they're taking on too much, it can lead to resentment.

- o Solution: Reassess and redistribute tasks. Use open communication to identify and address imbalances.

2. Different Standards

One partner may have higher expectations for cleanliness or organization than the other.

- o Solution: Find a compromise that respects both perspectives, or assign tasks accordingly.

3. Resistance to Change

If one partner is used to a traditional division of labor, it may take time to adjust.

- **Solution:** Approach the topic with patience and understanding, emphasizing how sharing responsibilities benefits both of you.

Sharing Responsibilities in Action

1. Household Chores

- Alternate cooking dinner or cleaning up afterward.

- Schedule a weekly "power hour" where you both tackle housework together.

2. Financial Responsibilities

- Set up monthly budgeting meetings to review expenses and goals.

- Divide financial tasks, such as one partner handling day-to-day bills while the other focuses on long-term savings.

3. Parenting

- Share bedtime routines or alternate school drop-offs and pickups.

- Collaborate on parenting strategies, ensuring both voices are heard.

4. Emotional Support

- Be attentive to your wife's emotional needs and encourage her to do the same for you.

- Share the responsibility of checking in on each other's well-being regularly.

5. Relationship Maintenance

- Plan date nights together, taking turns deciding on activities.

- Share the work of remembering and celebrating important milestones like anniversaries or birthdays.

The Role of Empathy in Sharing Responsibilities

Approach responsibilities with empathy and understanding. Recognize when your wife might be feeling overwhelmed, and be willing to step in to help. Likewise, communicate your needs clearly when you're feeling burdened.

By being empathetic, you create an environment where both partners feel supported and valued, strengthening your partnership.

Reflection Questions

- Are the responsibilities in your marriage currently balanced?

- How can you improve communication about shared tasks?

- What steps can you take to make sharing responsibilities feel more collaborative and less burdensome?

Sharing responsibilities is more than just dividing tasks—it's about building a partnership rooted in mutual respect, empathy, and teamwork. When both partners actively contribute to the relationship and household, it creates a sense of fairness and harmony that benefits both individuals and the marriage as a whole.

By approaching responsibilities with love and collaboration, you create a marriage where both partners feel valued, supported, and united in building a life together. Remember, the goal is not perfection but partnership—a shared journey where both of you work together to navigate the challenges and joys of married life.

Chapter 7
PURSUE HER PASSIONATELY

"Let your fountain be blessed, and rejoice in the wife of your youth." (Proverbs 5:18)

The passion in marriage is not limited to romantic love or physical intimacy—it encompasses emotional connection, shared dreams, and a deep, ongoing desire to cherish and honor your wife. Pursuing your wife passionately means continuously showing her love, affection, and admiration, regardless of how many years you've been married. It means keeping the fire of desire alive, not only in the bedroom but in every aspect of your relationship. In other words, you must be able to make love to her without even touching her. It should be mentally and emotionally first. Once you have mastered that, there is nothing she would not do for you.

In a world where distractions and busy schedules often take priority, pursuing your wife passionately is an intentional and deliberate act. It requires effort, consistency, and a heart that genuinely seeks to make her feel special, wanted, and deeply loved. The key to a passionate marriage is not merely relying on past efforts or memories of "the honeymoon phase" but actively pursuing your wife as if you're still courting her every day.

The Importance of Pursuing Your Wife Passionately

1. **Keeps the Spark Alive:** A passionate pursuit nurtures the romance and affection that initially brought you together.

2. **Affirms Her Worth:** Regularly pursuing your wife shows her that she is still your priority, that she is treasured, and that she holds an irreplaceable place in your life.

3. **Strengthens Emotional and Physical Connection:** A passionate pursuit deepens both emotional intimacy and physical closeness, creating a healthy, thriving marriage.

What Does It Mean to Pursue Your Wife Passionately?

Pursuing your wife passionately means engaging in acts that foster a deep emotional connection, offering continual affection, and finding new ways to express your love and desire for her. It is a marriage mindset that fuels romance, keeps you both emotionally engaged, and allows you to continue growing together as partners. Here's how you can pursue your wife passionately:

1. **Romantic Gestures:** Continue to woo your wife as you did in the early stages of dating—surprise her with thoughtful acts of love, whether it's a spontaneous date night, a hand-written note, or small acts of service.

2. **Words of Affirmation:** Regularly express your admiration and love through kind words, compliments, and encouragement. Let her know she is still the woman you adore.

3. **Physical Affection:** Physical touch is a powerful way to convey love. Hold hands, kiss often, and show affection both in private and in public.

4. **Cherish Her Spirit and Mind:** Pursue her intellectually and emotionally as well, by engaging in meaningful conversations, sharing your dreams, and being genuinely interested in her thoughts, desires, and feelings.

5. **Be Intentional About Quality Time:** Spend time together doing things that bring joy and strengthen your bond—whether it's a shared hobby, a weekend getaway, or simply enjoying a quiet evening at home.

Practical Ways to Pursue Your Wife Passionately

1. Keep the Romance Alive

Romance doesn't end after the wedding day—it should continue to flourish throughout the entirety of your marriage. Your pursuit of romance should evolve as your relationship matures, creating new ways to make your wife feel loved and appreciated.

Scripture:

"Let all that you do be done in love." (1 Corinthians 16:14)

Application:

- Plan regular date nights, even if they're simple or at home.

- Write her love letters or leave sweet notes for her to find.

- Show thoughtfulness in the small, everyday things that convey how much you care.

2. Be Her Biggest Cheerleader

Passion in marriage extends beyond physical affection to emotional support. Show your wife that you are fully invested in her well-being and success. Celebrate her accomplishments, encourage her dreams, and provide unwavering support as she pursues her goals.

Scripture:

"A wife of noble character who can find? She is worth far more than rubies." (Proverbs 31:10)

Application:

- Take time to acknowledge her achievements, whether big or small, and praise her efforts.

- Support her endeavors, whether they relate to career, personal growth, or ministry.

- Offer prayers for her strength, guidance, and success in all areas of life.

3. Foster Emotional Intimacy

Passion thrives in an emotionally connected marriage. Share your thoughts, feelings, and experiences with your wife regularly to keep your emotional bond strong. Encourage her to open up as well, creating a space where both of you feel heard, understood, and valued.

Scripture:

"The man who has friends must himself be friendly." (Proverbs 18:24)

Application:

- Take time to listen to your wife without distraction or judgment.

- Share your dreams, struggles, and joys with her, and ask about hers.

- Offer emotional support, affirm her feelings, and be present when she needs someone to lean on.

4. Be Physically Present and Affectionate

While words and gestures are important, physical touch is a powerful way to communicate love and passion. Affection shouldn't just be reserved for the bedroom—it should be part of your everyday interactions. Hold hands, hug, kiss, and show affection in ways that make her feel valued and loved.

Scripture:

"Let your fountain be blessed, and rejoice in the wife of your youth." (Proverbs 5:18)

Application:

- Initiate physical touch regularly, whether it's a kiss, an embrace, or simply holding hands.

- Offer hugs during stressful times or when she needs comfort.

- Ensure that intimacy in the bedroom remains a priority, continually nurturing that connection with love, care, and sensitivity.

5. Prioritize Her Needs

To pursue your wife passionately means putting her needs at the forefront of your mind. This includes both her practical and emotional needs. When you prioritize her, you demonstrate your deep care and commitment to her well-being.

Scripture:

"Husbands, love your wives, just as Christ loved the church and gave himself up for her." (Ephesians 5:25)

Application:

- Be attentive to her emotional needs, and offer comfort when she's feeling down or stressed.

- Help with household responsibilities or parenting duties when she needs a break.

- Listen attentively when she talks, showing that her thoughts and feelings are important to you.

Challenges to Pursuing Your Wife Passionately

1. **Complacency:** Over time, it's easy to become complacent and stop actively pursuing your wife as you did in the early days.

2. **Distractions:** The busyness of life, work, and family responsibilities can sometimes distract you from showing your wife love and affection.

3. **Miscommunication:** Sometimes, your wife's emotional or physical needs might not align with your understanding, leading to frustration or unmet expectations.

How to Overcome These Challenges:

- Be intentional about prioritizing your wife and your relationship.

- Set aside distractions like phones or work to fully focus on her.

- Communicate openly with your wife about her needs and desires, and actively listen to her.

Scriptural Inspiration for Pursuing Your Wife Passionately

- *"Let your fountain be blessed, and rejoice in the wife of your youth." (Proverbs 5:18)*

This verse encourages husbands to take joy in their wives and continually cherish them, nurturing passion throughout the years.

- *"And walk in love, as Christ also has loved us and given Himself for us, an offering and a sacrifice to God for a sweet-smelling aroma." (Ephesians 5:2)*

Christ's love for the church is sacrificial and enduring—this same love should guide how you pursue your wife with passion and devotion.

Reflection Questions

- How can I reignite the romance in my marriage and pursue my wife with intentionality?

- What small gestures can I incorporate into my daily routine to show my wife she is desired and loved?

- How can I deepen our emotional connection and foster greater intimacy in our marriage?

Affection is important to women. Especially to the women designed to be a wife. Affection to a wife shows her that you love, honor, respect, care for and want her and only her. Affection is hugs, kisses, holding of the hand(s), gazing into her beautiful eyes, and a gentle touch as you are near her. I had to learn and still are learning what my wife needed/wanted. It took me years to properly cater to her.

Pursuing your wife passionately is not a one-time act but an ongoing commitment to show her love, respect, and desire. By nurturing both the emotional and physical aspects of your marriage, you will keep the flame of passion alive and create a deep, lasting bond.

Remember that true passion is not just about grand gestures or fleeting moments but about consistently showing up for your wife in meaningful ways. When you pursue her passionately, you reflect the love Christ has for His church, making your marriage a beautiful example of sacrificial love, intimacy, and joy.

Bonus: Prioritize Quality Time

The Gift of Presence

In the busyness of life, it can be easy for quality time to slip down the list of priorities. Between work, family obligations, and personal responsibilities, many couples find themselves sharing space but not true connection. However, prioritizing quality time with your husband is essential to maintaining intimacy, building trust, and strengthening your bond. It's a reminder that, amidst everything else, your relationship remains a priority.

Why Quality Time Matters

Quality time is not just about being in the same room—it's about giving each other undivided attention and creating moments that deepen your connection. It provides the opportunity to learn more about each other, nurture emotional intimacy, and simply enjoy being together. When you prioritize quality time, you communicate to your husband that he matters to you and that your relationship is worth investing in.

Key Benefits of Quality Time:

- Strengthens emotional and physical intimacy.
- Reduces stress and provides a sense of support.
- Creates shared memories and experiences.
- Promotes better communication and understanding.
- Reinforces your commitment to each other.

Practical Ways to Prioritize Quality Time

1. Schedule It Intentionally

In a world filled with obligations, quality time doesn't always happen spontaneously—it needs to be planned.

- **Set a Weekly Date Night:** Designate a specific day each week for just the two of you. It doesn't have to be elaborate; even a cozy night at home can be meaningful.

- **Block Time in Your Calendar:** Treat quality time as non-negotiable by adding it to your schedule, just like any other important commitment.

- **Plan Mini Getaways:** Every so often, plan a weekend trip or staycation to reconnect away from daily distractions.

2. Make Everyday Moments Count

Quality time doesn't always require grand gestures. Sometimes, the most meaningful moments happen in the mundane.

- **Cook or Eat Together:** Preparing meals together can be a bonding experience, and sharing a meal without distractions fosters conversation.

- **Run Errands as a Team:** Turn routine tasks into an opportunity to spend time together by grocery shopping or running errands as a pair.

- **Wind Down Together:** At the end of the day, spend a few minutes talking, cuddling, or simply enjoying each other's presence before bed.

3. Disconnect to Reconnect

Technology can be one of the biggest barriers to quality time. Make a conscious effort to unplug and focus solely on each other.

- **Set Phone-Free Zones:** Create times or spaces where phones and devices are off-limits, like during dinner or date nights.

- **Limit Screen Time Together:** Instead of watching TV every night or being buried in your phone, opt for activities that encourage interaction, like playing a game or having a conversation.

4. Engage in Activities You Both Enjoy

Shared hobbies and interests create opportunities for fun, teamwork, and connection.

- **Try New Things Together:** Whether it's cooking a new recipe, taking a dance class, or trying an outdoor activity, exploring something new as a couple strengthens your bond.

- **Revisit Old Favorites:** Think back to activities you enjoyed early in your relationship, like hiking, watching a certain genre of movies, or playing a sport.

- **Support Each Other's Interests:** Even if you don't share the same hobbies, taking an interest in what your husband loves can be a meaningful way to spend time together.

5. Prioritize Conversation Over Tasks

Often, couples get caught up discussing logistics—like bills, schedules, and household chores—at the expense of meaningful conversation.

- **Ask Open-Ended Questions:** Encourage deeper dialogue with questions like, "What's been on your mind lately?" or "What's something you're excited about?"

- **Reflect on Your Relationship:** Discuss your shared dreams, goals, and memories to foster intimacy.

- **Practice Active Listening:** Show genuine interest in what your husband shares, without interrupting or multitasking.

Overcoming Challenges to Quality Time

1. Busy Schedules

Time is one of the most valuable resources, and it often feels in short supply. However, prioritizing your marriage means carving out time for it, even in a packed schedule.

- **Start Small:** Even 15 minutes of focused attention can make a difference.

- **Multitask Meaningfully:** Turn everyday activities, like walking the dog or folding laundry, into quality time by doing them together and engaging in conversation.

2. Fatigue or Stress

After a long day, it's tempting to retreat into individual routines. Combat this by prioritizing restorative, low-effort activities.

- **Opt for Relaxation Together:** Spend time unwinding together with a quiet activity, like reading side by side or listening to music.

- **Be Honest About Your Needs:** If you're too tired for a planned activity, communicate openly and find a simpler way to connect.

3. Lack of Alignment on Interests

It's okay if you and your husband don't share all the same hobbies or preferences.

- **Alternate Choices:** Take turns choosing activities so both of you feel included and valued.

- **Focus on the Experience:** Even if the activity isn't your favorite, enjoy the opportunity to spend time together and support his interests.

The Role of Quality Time in Building Intimacy

Quality time fosters emotional, physical, and spiritual intimacy. When you make space for undistracted connection, you strengthen the trust and closeness that form the foundation of your marriage. Over time, these moments become cherished memories and a testament to your shared commitment.

Reflection Questions

- When was the last time you and your husband spent uninterrupted time together?

- What are some activities or routines you can incorporate to create more quality time?

- How can you show your husband that time with him is a priority?

You can strengthen your bond, deepen intimacy, and improve communication by intentionally setting aside time for dates. Life is busy, with children, work, and other responsibilities often pulling your attention in different directions. If you're not careful, these distractions can strain your relationship. Date nights are a way to reconnect and show your wife that she matters and is deserving of your time and effort.

Here's a little secret: date nights don't have to be expensive or elaborate, and you don't always have to go out. My wife and I make it a priority to date often, and I take joy in planning most of our dates because I'm excited to spend quality time with her. Sometimes, we go out for dinner, catch a movie, or try something new, but some of my favorite date nights are the ones we have at home. I get creative and focus on making the experience special.

When planning a date, it's important to include your wife in the process—this doesn't mean she has to do the planning but that her preferences and interests are at the center of the experience. Pay attention to what she loves and incorporate that into your plans. Don't plan dates with the expectation of getting something in return, such as physical intimacy. Your wife longs for emotional intimacy first, and date nights are an excellent way to fulfill that need.

Date nights are not just about the activity—they're about having fun and enjoying each other's company. This is essential for keeping your relationship strong and healthy. The key is to make the time special and meaningful for your wife. While surprises are great, ensure they reflect her desires, not just what you assume she'll like.

I've learned this lesson firsthand. Early on, I planned several dates based on what I thought my wife would enjoy, only to realize later that they were more about me than her. While she didn't dislike the dates, they didn't truly resonate with her. I've since learned to plan with her in mind, focusing on what makes her feel valued and loved.

There are countless ways to enjoy date nights—take a walk in the park, watch the sunset, sit by the water, go out to eat, or cook dinner together at home. Don't limit yourselves to the same routines; try new things and stay open to creativity. The key is to make each date intentional and reflective of your wife's needs and interests. A meaningful date night will strengthen your bond and remind her of how much she means to you.

Quality time is an investment in the health and happiness of your marriage. It doesn't require lavish dates or grand plans—it simply requires your presence, attention, and willingness to connect. By prioritizing moments of togetherness, you nurture the bond that keeps your relationship strong and vibrant, even in the midst of life's challenges.

When you make time for each other, you reaffirm your love and commitment in the most meaningful way possible. Let your shared moments be a celebration of the life and love you've built together.

Chapter 8

SUPPORT HER CALLING AND ASSIGNMENTS FROM GOD

"I praise you because I am fearfully and wonderfully made; your works are wonderful, I know that full well." (Psalm 139:14)

In every marriage, one of the most profound ways a husband can love his wife is by actively supporting her divine calling and assignments from God. Every person, including your wife, is created with a unique purpose, and as her husband, you are called to be her biggest advocate and encourager in fulfilling that purpose. Whether her calling is in ministry, career, motherhood, or a specific area of service, your support can empower her to walk confidently in God's plan for her life.

Supporting your wife in her God-given calling requires understanding, encouragement, and active participation. It means helping her prioritize her divine assignments and providing the resources, time, and space she needs to pursue them. It also involves praying for her strength, wisdom, and clarity as she steps out in faith. Supporting your wife's calling demonstrates a deep respect for her as an individual with unique gifts and talents, and it aligns with God's desire for both of you to thrive in your respective roles and callings as a married couple.

The Importance of Supporting Her Calling

1. **God's Purpose for Her Life:** Supporting your wife in her calling is an acknowledgment that God has a unique purpose for her, and you honor that purpose by encouraging her to fulfill it.

2. **Strengthening Your Marriage:** When both spouses are actively working in alignment with God's will, it strengthens the foundation of the marriage and fosters unity in Christ.

3. **Empowering Her to Grow Spiritually and Personally:** Supporting her calling helps her grow in confidence, deepens her

relationship with God, and leads her to fulfill the potential God has placed within her.

What Does It Mean to Support Your Wife's Calling?

Supporting your wife's calling goes beyond simply acknowledging it—it requires active engagement and investment. It involves helping her discern God's voice, creating space for her to grow, and stepping in to lighten her load when necessary. Here's how you can support her in fulfilling her calling from God:

1. **Listen and Understand Her Calling:** Take the time to listen to your wife as she shares her dreams, passions, and sense of purpose. Help her discern what God is calling her to do.

2. **Pray for Her:** Prayer is one of the most powerful ways you can support your wife. Ask God to guide her steps, give her clarity, and equip her with everything she needs to fulfill her assignments.

3. **Encourage Her to Pursue Her Calling:** Be her greatest cheerleader. Offer words of encouragement, affirmation, and support, especially when she faces doubts or challenges.

4. **Provide Practical Support:** Sometimes, supporting your wife means helping her with the practical aspects of her calling, whether that's taking on more household responsibilities, creating a quiet space for her to work, or even helping her balance her schedule.

5. **Help Her Set Priorities:** Encourage your wife to focus on what God has called her to do, while also helping her manage her time and energy so that she can pursue her calling without becoming overwhelmed.

Practical Ways to Support Your Wife's Calling

1. Be Her Spiritual Partner

Your wife's calling is intricately connected to her relationship with God. As her husband, you are her spiritual partner, and together, you are called to walk in faith. Pray together for wisdom, direction, and strength as she navigates her calling. Encourage her to seek God's will through His Word and trust in His plan for her life.

Scripture:

"Two are better than one, because they have a good return for their labor: If either of them falls down, one can help the other up." (Ecclesiastes 4:9-10)

Application:

- Spend time in prayer together, seeking God's will for her calling.

- Share spiritual insights and encourage one another to grow in faith.

- Celebrate the spiritual milestones and victories in her journey.

2. Create Space for Her Calling

Every calling requires time and space to grow and flourish. As her husband, help her find the time and resources to fully embrace and pursue what God has called her to do. This may mean adjusting schedules, reducing distractions, or stepping in to help with responsibilities so that she can devote her energy to her assignment.

Scripture:

"But Martha was distracted by all the preparations that had to be made. She came to him and asked, 'Lord, don't you care that my sister has left me to do the work by myself? Tell her to help me!' 'Martha, Martha,' the Lord answered, 'you are worried and upset about many things, but few things are needed—or indeed only one. Mary has chosen what is better, and it will not be taken away from her.'" (Luke 10:40-42)

Application:

- Encourage your wife to make time for her calling by offering to take on tasks or responsibilities she may not have the time for.

- Create an environment where she can focus on what God has called her to do without feeling overwhelmed by everyday distractions.

- Be patient and understanding if her calling requires sacrifices from both of you.

3. Support Her Through Challenges

The journey of fulfilling God's calling is often filled with obstacles and challenges. Your support is vital when she faces setbacks, doubts, or discouragement. Be a source of strength and encouragement, reminding her of God's promises and that He is with her every step of the way.

Scripture:

"I can do all this through him who gives me strength." *(Philippians 4:13)*

Application:

- Encourage her when she's discouraged and help her refocus on God's purpose.

- Offer practical help and emotional support during difficult times.

- Remind her of the promises in Scripture and that God equips those He calls.

4. Celebrate Her Achievements and Progress

Celebrate the milestones in your wife's journey of fulfilling her calling. Recognizing her achievements—whether big or small—lets her know you value her efforts and are proud of her growth. Take time to acknowledge her hard work, and be her loudest supporter.

Scripture:

"Rejoice with those who rejoice; mourn with those who mourn." *(Romans 12:15)*

Application:

- Acknowledge and celebrate her accomplishments in her calling, no matter how small they may seem.

- Show genuine excitement and gratitude for her work and the way she is following God's leading.

- Make it a point to encourage her when she achieves new goals or makes progress in her assignments.

5. Trust Her and Empower Her to Lead

One of the most important ways to support your wife is by trusting in her ability to fulfill her calling. Empower her to take the lead in areas where she excels, and honor the gifts God has given her. Trust that she can make wise decisions, and stand by her as she takes action on the assignments God has placed before her.

Scripture:

"She speaks with wisdom, and faithful instruction is on her tongue." (Proverbs 31:26)

Application:

- Give her the space to lead in areas related to her calling, whether it's in ministry, business, or the home.

- Encourage her to take ownership of her passions and talents, and trust that God will guide her.

- Be confident in her abilities and provide encouragement when she steps out in faith.

Challenges to Supporting Your Wife's Calling

1. **Time Constraints:** Balancing your own responsibilities with supporting her calling can be difficult.

2. **Feeling Inadequate:** You may sometimes feel like you don't have the resources or ability to help her fully fulfill her calling.

3. **Lack of Understanding:** At times, you may struggle to understand the full scope of her calling or why it's so important to her.

How to Overcome These Challenges:

- Communicate openly with your wife about how you can both prioritize her calling and manage time effectively.

- Trust in God's ability to equip both of you with what is needed to fulfill His will.

- Take time to learn more about her calling and how you can best support it.

Scriptural Inspiration for Supporting Her Calling

- *"But the one who calls you is faithful, and he will do it." (1 Thessalonians 5:24)*

God is faithful to fulfill His purpose in your wife's life, and you are called to be a vessel of support as she walks in obedience to His will.

- *"As each has received a gift, use it to serve one another, as good stewards of God's varied grace." (1 Peter 4:10)*

Every person has unique gifts and callings. Supporting your wife is an acknowledgment that she is stewarding her gifts and talents to serve both God and others.

Reflection Questions

- How can I better understand and support my wife's divine calling?

- In what practical ways can I help her find time and space to pursue her calling?

- How can I empower my wife to confidently lead and pursue her passions?

Supporting your wife's calling is an act of love and obedience to God's design for your marriage. It requires intentional listening, prayer, and active involvement in helping her fulfill her divine assignments. When you support her in her calling, you are not only honoring her but also honoring God's will for your marriage and family.

Remember, your wife's calling is beautiful!

Chapter 9

COVER HER AND PROTECT HER HEART

"Above all else, guard your heart, for everything you do flows from it." (Proverbs 4:23)

In marriage, one of the most important ways a husband can love his wife is by protecting her heart—emotionally, spiritually, and mentally. A husband who covers his wife creates a safe environment in which she feels cherished, valued, and secure. This protection is not merely about shielding her from external harm, but also guarding her from emotional and spiritual distress, offering reassurance in times of vulnerability, and being a constant source of support when challenges arise.

Protecting your wife's heart is about more than just physical safety; it's about being her emotional safeguard, ensuring she feels deeply respected, supported, and loved. As her husband, you are called to be a protector of her inner being, helping to create a space where she can heal, grow, and thrive. By honoring and covering her heart, you create a foundation of trust and security that strengthens the bond between you and allows your relationship to flourish.

Why Protecting Her Heart Matters

1. **Emotional Security:** A wife who feels emotionally protected and cared for is more likely to open up, be vulnerable, and share her innermost thoughts and feelings with you.

2. **Spiritual Safety:** A wife needs spiritual protection, encouragement, and guidance as she walks out her faith. When you provide a safe space for her spiritually, you allow her to grow closer to God and pursue her own relationship with Him.

3. **Encouragement to Be Herself:** Protecting her heart allows her to express herself fully, knowing that her emotions, needs, and desires will be respected and cared for.

What It Means to Cover and Protect Her Heart

1. **Guard Her from Harmful Words and Actions:** Words have the power to build up or tear down. As her protector, guard her from hurtful words—whether from others or even from yourself. Encourage and speak life into her heart, and be mindful of how your actions and words impact her emotional well-being.

2. **Be Her Emotional Support:** When life becomes difficult, your wife needs a safe space to express her fears, frustrations, and doubts without feeling judged. Be her listener, her confidant, and her emotional support. When she shares her heart, listen with empathy and understanding, not with the desire to fix everything immediately.

3. **Shield Her from Unnecessary Stress and Worry:** Part of protecting her heart involves reducing unnecessary burdens on her shoulders. Take on responsibilities or tasks that might add stress to her life, and proactively look for ways to ease her load.

4. **Respect Her Vulnerability:** Vulnerability is essential in a marriage, but it requires a safe environment to flourish. When your wife is open and vulnerable with you, protect her trust by showing compassion, understanding, and patience. Don't use her vulnerability against her. Instead, hold her heart with care, allowing it to flourish.

5. **Lead with Love and Gentleness:** Lead your marriage with a gentle and loving heart, especially when difficult conversations arise. Speak with kindness and patience, avoiding harsh tones or actions. A wife who feels safe with her husband will be more willing to face difficult situations and grow in the relationship.

Biblical Foundation for Protecting Her Heart

The Bible speaks often about the importance of guarding one's heart, and this principle extends to your wife's heart as well. Proverbs 4:23 is a reminder that everything flows from the heart. As her husband, you are entrusted with the responsibility to help keep her heart free from unnecessary distress, pain, and negativity. By doing so, you protect the sanctity and health of your marriage.

Scripture:

"Husbands, love your wives, just as Christ loved the church and gave himself up for her." (Ephesians 5:25)

Application:

Just as Christ laid down His life for the church, a husband is called to sacrificially love his wife. Part of that sacrificial love is protecting her heart, which includes guarding her against emotional harm and ensuring that she feels safe and cherished in the relationship.

Practical Ways to Protect Her Heart

1. Be Her Protector in All Circumstances

Protecting your wife's heart means shielding her from unnecessary negativity, criticism, or harmful influences. If she is facing challenges in her relationships, work, or outside world, be her first line of defense. Be the one who stands up for her, defends her, and shields her from people or situations that could harm her emotionally.

Scripture:

"Let no unwholesome talk come out of your mouths, but only what is helpful for building others up according to their needs, that it may benefit those who listen." (Ephesians 4:29)

Application:

- Speak words of encouragement and affirmation into her life.
- Defend her honor when others speak negatively of her.
- Shield her from gossip, criticism, or negativity from others.

2. Be Her Safe Place for Vulnerability

Creating an environment where your wife feels safe to express her true emotions is essential. Allow her to be vulnerable without fear of judgment or condemnation. When she shares her struggles, be patient, listen intently, and offer words of comfort and reassurance.

Scripture:

"A gentle answer turns away wrath, but a harsh word stirs up anger." (Proverbs 15:1)

Application:

- Let her speak freely about her emotions without interrupting or trying to "fix" the situation.

- Respond with gentleness and understanding when she is vulnerable.

- Show empathy by validating her feelings and offering emotional support.

3. Practice Patience and Understanding

Protecting her heart involves being patient when times are tough or when she is facing emotional challenges. Understand that emotional wounds can take time to heal, and sometimes the best thing you can do is offer your steady presence and patience.

Scripture:

"Be completely humble and gentle; be patient, bearing with one another in love." (Ephesians 4:2)

Application:

- Be patient when she is processing emotions or difficult situations.

- Show understanding when she needs time to heal or cope with her struggles.

- Offer quiet support, even when you may not have all the answers.

4. Be Her Spiritual Shield

Spiritual protection is just as important as emotional protection. Guard her heart spiritually by praying for her, encouraging her in her faith, and helping her navigate challenges in her relationship with God. Remind her of God's promises and offer her strength when her faith is tested.

Scripture:

"The Lord will fight for you; you need only to be still." (Exodus 14:14)

Application:

- Pray over your wife, asking God to protect her heart from spiritual attacks and discouragement.

- Be her spiritual companion by praying together, reading Scripture, and worshiping God together.

- Help her stay grounded in her faith when external pressures threaten to overwhelm her.

5. Offer Reassurance and Security

To protect her heart, provide reassurance and security in your relationship. This includes offering emotional consistency and reliability, being there when she needs you, and letting her know that you are committed to her, no matter the challenges that come your way.

Scripture:

"Though the mountains be shaken and the hills be removed, yet my unfailing love for you will not be shaken." (Isaiah 54:10)

Application:

- Reassure her of your commitment and love regularly, especially during times of trial.

- Be reliable in your words and actions so she knows she can trust you with her heart.

- Show her through your actions that you are her steadfast source of security and love.

Reflection Questions

- In what ways can I better protect my wife's heart emotionally and spiritually?

- How can I be more patient and understanding when she shares her feelings?

- What are some practical ways I can shield her from unnecessary stress or harm?

Covering your wife is a vital aspect of marriage and an essential part of her well-being. Women naturally crave security, protection, and love, and as a husband, it is your responsibility to provide these things. Covering your wife means being her head, her guide, and her frontline. It does not mean controlling, hindering, or blocking her growth. Instead, it signifies the spiritual and emotional protection you provide as her partner under God's design.

The concept of covering a wife is rooted in biblical principles. As her husband, you are called to be her spiritual leader, providing guidance and protection. Covering your wife involves loving her as Christ loves the church, nurturing her, and ensuring her safety—physically, emotionally, and spiritually. I want to share some insights into what it means for a husband to spiritually cover his wife because, honestly, I've made mistakes in this area.

There were times I failed to cover my wife properly. I allowed others, even people in the church, to speak negatively about her without stepping in to defend her. I neglected to pray with and for her. I didn't wash her with the Word of God, and when someone else did, I became upset—not because they were wrong, but because I had failed in my role as her spiritual covering. My wife expressed her hurt and frustration about these things, but I ignored her cries. Husbands, I urge you to listen to your wife's needs and emotions before it's too late.

The Bible speaks of covering both implicitly and explicitly. In 1 Corinthians 11:1-16, we see that covering is not just about a physical or symbolic act but about leadership and responsibility. Adam's failure to cover Eve in the Garden of Eden had devastating consequences (Genesis 3). Adam was placed in the garden to tend and protect it (Genesis 2), yet when the serpent approached, he failed to guard his wife from deception. This teaches us that the role of covering is not passive but active and intentional.

Husbands, we are charged by God to stand as the head and leader of our wives. As 1 Corinthians 11:3 reminds us, "The head of every man is Christ, and the head of the woman is man, and the head of Christ is God." To lead effectively, we must first allow God to lead us. When we are submitted to God, we can guide our wives with love, wisdom, and strength.

One of the key ways we cover our wives is by speaking life into them. Proverbs 18:21 reminds us, "The tongue has the power of life and death." Every word we speak has the potential to either build up or tear down. This includes words spoken in moments of tiredness, anger, frustration, or disappointment. As husbands, we are called to ensure that our words breathe life into our wives and our marriage. A godly husband uses his tongue to nurture and encourage his wife, not to harm her.

Ultimately, covering your wife means being her protector, advocate, and spiritual support. Pray with her and for her. Speak words of affirmation and encouragement over her. Lead her with humility and love, allowing God to direct your steps. Remember, being a covering for your wife is not just an option; it is a biblical mandate given to us by God. Let us fulfill this sacred duty with honor and devotion, reflecting God's love in every aspect of our marriage.

Protecting your wife's heart is one of the most profound ways you can love her. By guarding her emotions, offering spiritual support, and providing a safe space for vulnerability, you create a marriage built on trust, safety, and unconditional love. As her husband, you are called to cover her heart with the same care and commitment that Christ shows to the Church. When you protect her heart, you allow her to flourish in the fullness of who God created her to be, and together, you build a relationship rooted in deep love and respect.

Chapter 10

WASHING HER WITH THE WORD OF GOD

"Husbands, love your wives, just as Christ loved the church and gave Himself up for her to make her holy, cleansing her by the washing with water through the word." (Ephesians 5:25-26)

As a husband, one of the most powerful ways you can love your wife is by "washing her with the Word of God." This means spiritually nurturing her through Scripture, prayer, and godly counsel. Just as Christ nourishes and sanctifies the church through His Word, so should a husband nourish and encourage his wife through the truth of God's Word. By doing so, you contribute to her spiritual growth, her emotional well-being, and her overall sense of peace and security.

The Word of God is alive and powerful (Hebrews 4:12), and it has the ability to heal, renew, and transform. When you speak Scripture over your wife, share spiritual insights, or pray the Word with her, you are actively participating in her sanctification and growth in Christ. This nurturing act goes beyond mere encouragement; it is a divine investment into her soul.

Why Washing Her with the Word Matters

1. **Spiritual Growth:** Just as your wife needs physical nourishment to thrive, she also requires spiritual nourishment. Washing her with the Word means actively helping her grow deeper in her relationship with God. A wife whose husband invests in her spiritual development is more likely to have a stronger and more fulfilling walk with God.

2. **Emotional Healing:** The Word of God is a source of comfort and healing. When your wife faces struggles—whether emotional, mental, or spiritual—Scripture can offer the peace and reassurance she needs to overcome. A husband who washes his wife with the Word helps her to deal with life's difficulties through the lens of God's truth.

3. **Building a Stronger Marriage:** A marriage grounded in the Word of God is one that stands strong, even in the face of trials. When you both turn to Scripture in your marriage, you build a solid foundation that is rooted in divine wisdom and understanding. The Word has the power to bring unity, resolve conflict, and deepen the bond between you.

4. **Empowerment:** When you share God's promises with your wife, you empower her to live in the fullness of her identity in Christ. You remind her of her worth and value in God's eyes, and you strengthen her faith as she faces the challenges of life.

How to Wash Her with the Word

1. **Pray Scripture Over Her:** Prayer is one of the most intimate ways you can nurture your wife spiritually. Pray Scripture over her regularly, asking God to work His Word in her life. Let Scripture guide your prayers, declaring God's promises over her health, her peace, her strength, and her purpose.

Example Scripture Prayers:

- *"Father, I pray that my wife would know the height, depth, and width of Your love for her, that she may be filled with the fullness of Your love (Ephesians 3:17-19)."*

- *"Lord, help my wife to be strong and courageous, not afraid or discouraged, for You are with her wherever she goes (Joshua 1:9)."*

2. **Speak Life into Her:** Words have immense power. Use your words to speak life, encouragement, and truth into her. Share Scripture with her that addresses her current struggles or uplifts her spirit. Remind her of God's promises and His love for her. When she is facing challenges, speak the Word over her to renew her mind and help her trust in God's plan.

Example Scripture Encouragement:

- *"My wife, remember that the Lord is your shepherd; you shall not want. He leads you beside still waters and restores your soul (Psalm 23:1-3)."*

- *"You are more than a conqueror through Him who loved you (Romans 8:37)."*

4. **Study the Word Together:** One of the most intimate ways you can wash your wife with the Word is by studying it together. Set aside time to read the Bible together, discuss its meaning, and apply it to your lives. This deepens your relationship not just with each other but with God as well. As you both reflect on the Word, you help each other grow in your faith and understanding.

5. **Encourage Her to Spend Time in the Word:** While you play an important role in washing her with the Word, your wife must also seek God on her own. Encourage her to spend time reading and meditating on Scripture. Offer to pray with her, support her in her personal Bible study, and remind her of the power of the Word in her life.

6. **Remind Her of God's Promises:** Life can be overwhelming, and we can easily forget God's promises in difficult times. As her husband, part of washing her with the Word is gently reminding her of what God has spoken over her. When she is discouraged, remind her of His faithfulness and the hope she has in Him.

Scripture Reminders:

- *"The Lord is your refuge and strength, an ever-present help in trouble (Psalm 46:1)."*

- *"For I know the plans I have for you, plans to prosper you and not to harm you, plans to give you a hope and a future (Jeremiah 29:11)."*

The Spiritual Role of a Husband in the Marriage

The Bible instructs husbands to love their wives as Christ loves the church (Ephesians 5:25). This means that your love for her should be sacrificial, unconditional, and nurturing. Christ not only loved the church by giving Himself for it but also by guiding it, teaching it, and sanctifying it with His Word. Similarly, a husband's role is to guide, nurture, and spiritually support his wife by speaking the truth of God's Word into her life.

By washing her with the Word, you take on a Christ-like role in her spiritual journey. This act of love requires intentionality, time, and prayer. But as you do this, you are fulfilling your God-given responsibility to love her in the way Christ has loved you, continually nourishing her soul and strengthening your marriage.

Biblical Foundation for Washing Her with the Word

The concept of washing with the Word comes directly from the Bible, where it is used in the context of how Christ loves and purifies the Church. In Ephesians 5:26-27, Paul teaches that Christ sanctifies and cleanses the Church by the washing of water through the Word, preparing it to be holy and blameless. Similarly, a husband is called to use the Word of God to sanctify his wife, to help her grow in holiness and spiritual strength. This is not merely a one-time act but an ongoing process of loving her with God's truth and leading her toward spiritual maturity.

Scripture:

"Husbands, love your wives, just as Christ loved the church and gave Himself up for her to make her holy, cleansing her by the washing with water through the word, and to present her to Himself as a radiant church, without stain or wrinkle or any other blemish, but holy and blameless." (Ephesians 5:25-27)

Application:

- Your words should bring about spiritual growth and transformation.

- Speak with love and grace, guiding your wife toward greater holiness.

- Allow God's Word to shape your marriage and relationship with your wife.

Washing your wife with the Word of God is one of the most profound ways to love and support her spiritually. It goes beyond just sharing Scripture—it's about nurturing her faith, speaking life and encouragement, and helping her grow in her relationship with God. As you fulfill this responsibility, you will build a marriage grounded in spiritual strength and mutual growth. Just as Christ nourishes the church, so should you nourish your wife with God's Word, continually guiding her toward holiness and helping her flourish in every area of life.

Conclusion
A LIFETIME OF LOVE

As we conclude this journey through ten essential ways to love your spouse and build a thriving marriage, it is important to remember that love is not just a feeling—it is a choice, an ongoing commitment, and an act of faith. The Scriptures provide timeless wisdom that, when applied, can transform the dynamics of any marriage. Whether it's loving unconditionally, listening attentively, leading with love, or practicing humility over pride, each principle is rooted in the foundation of God's Word and His design for marriage.

Marriage is a covenant, not just between two people but also with God. It is a relationship that thrives when both spouses commit to loving one another with the same sacrificial, unconditional love that Christ demonstrates toward His Church. As we put these principles into practice, we are not only honoring our spouse but also fulfilling God's purpose for our marriage. When we choose to love as God loves— through patience, humility, forgiveness, and grace—we are reflecting His image in a powerful way.

It's important to recognize that no marriage is perfect. There will be challenges, moments of tension, and times when we fail. But the beauty of a Christ-centered marriage is that we can always return to the source of love and strength—our Heavenly Father. His love is unshakable, His grace is abundant, and His presence can heal, restore, and renew our relationships.

As you continue your journey in marriage, remember that it is a lifelong process of growth, learning, and deepening intimacy. There will be seasons of joy and seasons of difficulty, but if you remain committed to nurturing your marriage with love, honor, and respect, you will build a relationship that stands the test of time.

May this book serve as a guide, a reminder, and an encouragement to always seek God's will in your marriage. May you grow together in faith, love, and unity, and may your marriage reflect the love of Christ to the world around you.

"Therefore what God has joined together, let no one separate." (Mark 10:9)

Let this truth be the anchor that keeps your marriage strong, fulfilling, and blessed by God. May you continue to love one another deeply, for love covers a multitude of sins and is the ultimate expression of God's heart for His people.

Blessings and grace to you both on this beautiful journey.

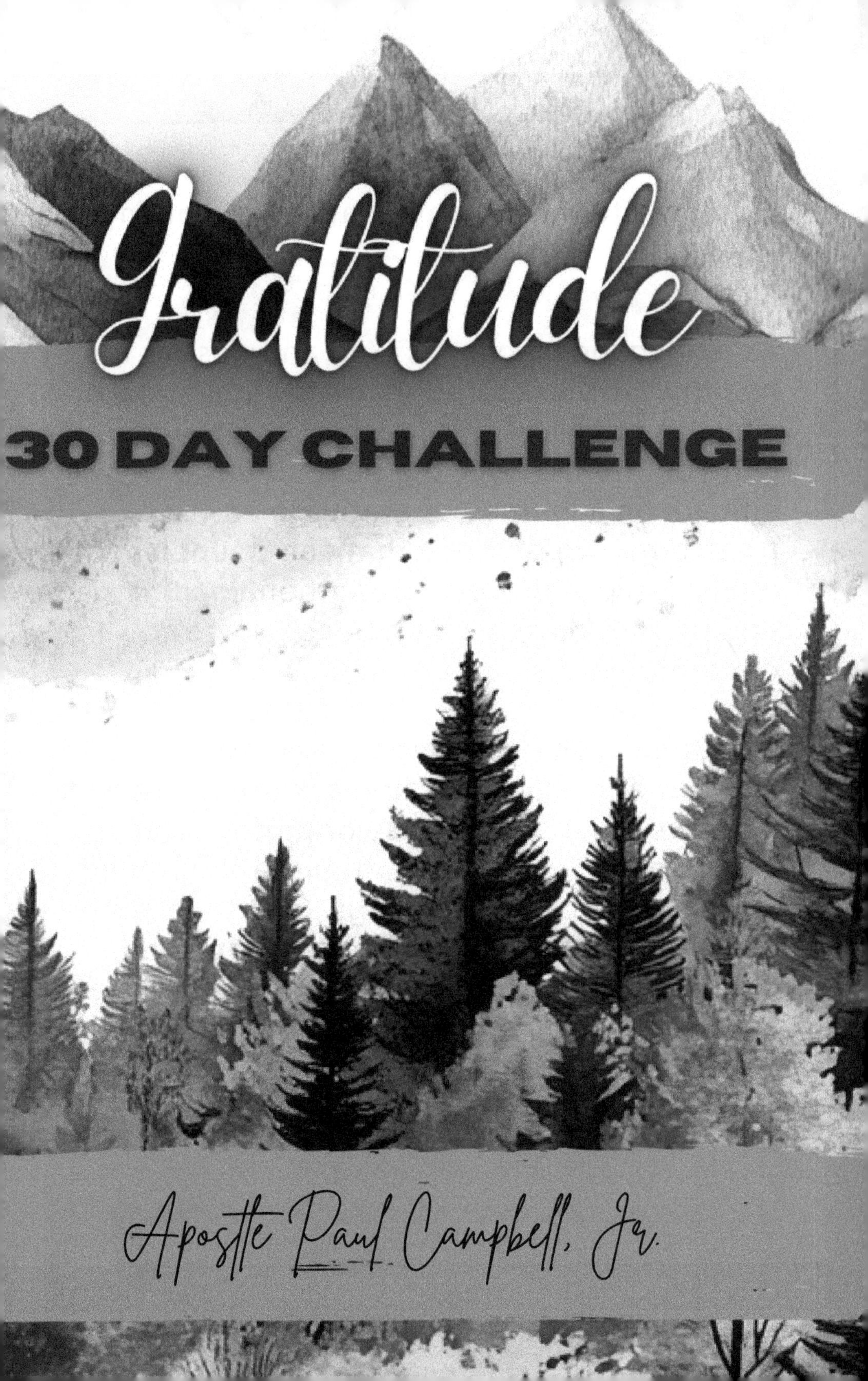
Gratitude
30 DAY CHALLENGE
Apostle Paul Campbell, Jr.

Welcome to the 30-Day Gratitude Challenge for Husbands!

As a husband who loves God and desires a healthy, God-centered marriage, you know how vital it is to keep Christ at the center of your life and your home. Over the next 30 days, we will embark on a journey of gratitude—a transformative practice that can deepen your relationship with God, strengthen your marriage, and fill your daily life with peace, joy, and contentment.

The Bible calls us to give thanks in all circumstances (1 Thessalonians 5:18). This isn't because life is always easy or perfect, but because we serve a God who is faithful, loving, and sovereign over all things. Gratitude shifts our focus from what's wrong to what God is doing, reminding us that His grace is sufficient and His plans are always for our good.

This devotional is designed to help you cultivate a heart of thankfulness through daily scripture reflections and practical action steps. Each day, you'll meditate on a Bible verse about thankfulness and consider how it applies to your life as a husband and a man of God. You'll also be encouraged to take intentional steps to express gratitude—not only to God but also to your wife, whose love and partnership are among God's greatest gifts to you.

Whether you're navigating challenges, enjoying a season of blessing, or simply seeking to grow in faith, this challenge will help you reframe your experiences through the lens of God's goodness. As you align your heart with His truth, you'll discover how gratitude can transform your mindset, renew your spirit, and strengthen your bond with your wife.

Through this challenge, you'll also learn to:

• Recognize and celebrate the blessings in your marriage.

• Speak life into your wife and encourage her with gratitude-filled words.

• Build a foundation of thankfulness that sustains your family through every season.

Prepare to experience God's presence in new and powerful ways as you commit to cultivating a grateful heart. Let's journey together, one day at a time, growing in thankfulness and discovering how a heart rooted in gratitude brings life to your faith, your marriage, and your family.

Let's begin this journey, honoring God and your wife, as we embrace the beauty of a grateful heart!

How It Works:

- Each day, you'll focus on a specific scripture that teaches us about gratitude.

- After reflecting on the scripture, you'll be invited to answer questions that help you think more deeply about how thankfulness can transform your life.

- Finally, you'll take a simple action step to put your gratitude into practice, allowing God's truth to impact the way you live.

Remember, this challenge is not about perfection but about progress. As you take time to meditate on God's Word and give thanks each day, you'll find your heart shifting towards joy and peace, no matter your circumstances. Let's get started on this life-changing journey of gratitude!

Apostle Paul Campbell, Jr.

the Power of Gratitude

1 Thessalonians 5:18 – "Give thanks in all circumstanc
for this is God's will for you in Christ Jesus."

Why is it important to give thanks in all situations? How can yo
start viewing your daily challenges as opportunities for growth?

Action Step: Write down three things you are thankful for today,
even in the midst of challenges.

_____

_____

_____

_____

_____

_____

_____

_____

_____

A Sacrifice of Praise

Hebrews 13:15 – "Through Jesus, therefore, let us continually offer to God a sacrifice of praise—the fruit of lips that openly profess his name."

How can you offer praise when life feels difficult? What might change if you intentionally choose gratitude in tough times?

Action Step: Offer a prayer of praise today for something you've been struggling with, thanking God for His presence in that situation.

_____

_____

_____

_____

_____

_____

_____

_____

_____

Thankfulness as a Shield Against Anxiety

Philippians 4:6-7 – "Do not be anxious about anythin but in every situation, by prayer and petition, with thanksgiving, present your requests to God." --

How does thankfulness help combat anxiety? How can you shift your focus from worry to God's faithfulness today?

Action Step: Whenever you feel anxious today, pause and thank God for one specific blessing. Repeat this throughout the day.

_____

_____

_____

_____

_____

_____

_____

_____

Colossians 3:15 – "Let the peace of Christ rule in your hearts, since as members of one body you were called to peace. And be thankful."

How does cultivating thankfulness bring peace to your heart? Where in your life do you need more of Christ's peace?

Action Step: Spend 5 minutes in quiet prayer, asking for God's peace to fill any areas of your heart where you lack it. Write down the things that you felt after praying.

_____

_____

_____

_____

_____

_____

_____

_____

_____

_____

_____

Gratitude and Humility

James 4:6 – "But He gives more grace. Therefore it says: 'God opposes the proud but gives grace to the humble

How does thankfulness keep you humble before God? How can you remember that all you have is from Him?

Action Step: Write a gratitude list that acknowledges how God has provided for you in specific areas of your life.

_____

_____

_____

_____

_____

_____

_____

_____

_____

Thankfulness in Prayer

Colossians 4:2 – "Devote yourselves to prayer, being watchful and thankful."

How does gratitude change the way you pray? Are there blessings you tend to overlook in your prayers?

Action Step: Incorporate thanksgiving into your prayers today. For every request you make, also give thanks for something God has already done.

_____

_____

_____

_____

_____

_____

_____

_____

Recognizing God's Goodness

Psalm 107:1 – "Give thanks to the Lord, for He is good; love endures forever."

How has God shown His goodness in your life? What can you thank Him for today that reflects His enduring love?

Action Step: Meditate on God's goodness and write a letter of gratitude to Him for His faithfulness in your life.

_____

_____

_____

_____

_____

_____

_____

_____

Colossians 2:6-7 – "So then, just as you received Christ Jesus as Lord, continue to live your lives in him... overflowing with thankfulness."

What would it look like to "overflow" with thankfulness in your daily life? How can you express gratitude for God's grace more often?

Action Step: Share with someone today something God has done in your life that fills you with gratitude.

_____

_____

_____

_____

_____

_____

_____

_____

_____

_____

_____

Thankfulness in Suffering

Romans 5:3-4 – "Not only that, but we rejoice in our sufferings, knowing that suffering produces endurance and endurance produces character, and character produces hope."

How does gratitude in suffering change your perspective? How has God strengthened your character through difficult times?

Action Step: Reflect on a past hardship and write down the way it has shaped you. Thank God for how He brought you through i

_____

_____

_____

_____

_____

_____

_____

_____

Psalm 34:1 – "I will bless the Lord at all times; His praise shall continually be in my mouth."

Is your heart quick to praise God in every circumstance? What habits can you build to maintain a heart of gratitude?

Action Step: Set a reminder on your phone to pause and praise God at least 3 times today for His goodness.

_____

_____

_____

_____

_____

_____

_____

_____

_____

_____

Giving Thanks in Prosperity and Lack

Philippians 4:12 – "I know what it is to be in need, an[d]
know what it is to have plenty... I have learned the se[cret]
of being content in any and every situation."

How can you practice contentment and thankfulness in bo[th]
abundance and need? How does this contentment refle[ct]
trust in God?

Action Step: Choose one area where you're discontent and
give thanks to God for what you do have in that area.

_____

_____

_____

_____

_____

_____

_____

_____

Thankfulness as Worship

Psalm 100:4 – "Enter His gates with thanksgiving and His courts with praise; give thanks to Him and praise His name."

How can thankfulness become an act of worship in your everyday life? How can you praise God for who He is, not just for what He's done?

Action Step: Turn on your favorite worship song today and sing along, focusing on God's attributes and expressing your gratitude.

_____

_____

_____

_____

_____

_____

_____

_____

_____

thankfulness and trust

Proverbs 3:5-6 – "Trust in the Lord with all your heart an
lean not on your own _understanding_."

How does trusting God in all circumstances help you develop
heart of gratitude? Where do you need to place more trust
God?

Action Step: Write down a situation where you're struggling to
trust God. Pray for His help, then give thanks in advance fo
how He will work it out.

_____

_____

_____

_____

_____

_____

_____

Psalm 16:11 – "You make known to me the path of life; you ~~will~~ fill me with joy in y~~our~~ presence."

How does focusing on God's blessings bring joy? What blessings can you meditate on today that will fill you with joy?

Action Step: Make a joy list by writing down at least 5 things that bring you joy because of God's blessings.

_____

_____

_____

_____

_____

_____

_____

_____

_____

the Example of Jesus

John 6:11 – "Jesus then took the loaves, gave thanks, a
distributed to those who were seated as much as the
___.wanted."

Why did Jesus give thanks before feeding the 5,000? How can
you give thanks before seeing the outcome in your life?

Action Step: Before eating your meals today, pause and give
thanks not only for the food but also for the unseen way:
God is working in your life.

_____

_____

_____

_____

_____

_____

_____

_____

_____

Corinthians 9:11 – "You will be enriched in every way so that you can be generous on every occasion, and through us your generosity will result in thanksgiving to God."

How does your thankfulness and generosity inspire others? How can you lead others to give thanks to God today?

Action Step: Perform a random act of kindness today, and let it point others toward gratitude for God's provision.

_____

_____

_____

_____

_____

_____

_____

_____

_____

Thankfulness in Small Things

Luke 16:10 – "Whoever can be trusted with very little c
also be trusted with much."

Are you thankful for the small blessings in life? How ca
recognizing the small things change your perspective on bigge
things?

Action Step: Take time today to thank God for the little things
you normally overlook (like running water, health, sunshine).

_____

_____

_____

_____

_____

_____

_____

_____

Philippians 2:14-15 – "Do everything without grumbling or arguing, so that you may become blameless and pure."

How does complaining affect your heart? What can you do today to stop grumbling and start giving thanks?

Action Step: Make a conscious effort to stop yourself from complaining today. When you feel the urge, replace it with a word of thanks instead.

_____

_____

_____

_____

_____

_____

_____

_____

_____

_____

Gratitude in Obedience

Deuteronomy 28:47 – "Because you did not serve the Lord your God joyfully and gladly in the time of prosperity."

How does joyful obedience reflect gratitude to God? How can you find joy in serving Him today?

Action Step: Find a way to serve someone today, whether big or small, and do it with a thankful heart.

_____

_____

_____

_____

_____

_____

_____

_____

Recognizing God's Faithfulness

Lamentations 3:22-23 – "Because of the Lord's great love we are not consumed, for His compassions never fail. They are new every morning; great is Your faithfulness."

How has God shown His faithfulness to you in the past? How can you thank Him for His faithfulness today and trust Him for tomorrow?

Action Step: Write a prayer of thanks to God, focusing on specific examples of His faithfulness in your life.

_____

_____

_____

_____

_____

_____

_____

_____

_____

Thankfulness for Salvation

Ephesians 2:8 – "For it is by grace you have been sav
through faith—and this is not from yourselves, it is th
gift of God."

How often do you thank God for the gift of salvation? How does
remembering this gift change your attitude in daily life?

Action Step: Take a moment today to thank God for His grace in
saving you, and reflect on how this impacts your everyday
actions.

_____

_____

_____

_____

_____

_____

_____

_____

A Grateful Heart is a Content Heart

1 Timothy 6:6 – "But godliness with contentment is great gain."

How does thankfulness produce contentment? What areas of your life do you need to surrender to God in order to find true contentment?

Action Step: Identify one area where you feel discontent and choose to give thanks instead of focusing on what you lack.

_____
_____
_____
_____
_____
_____
_____
_____

Matthew 5:44 – "But I tell you, love your enemies an
pray for those who persecute you."

How can you thank God for difficult relationships, knowing the
shape your character? How can you demonstrate Christ's love
these relationships?

Action Step: Pray for someone you are struggling with today
and ask God to give you a heart of gratitude for what He is
doing through that relationship.

_____

_____

_____

_____

_____

_____

_____

_____

Matthew 6:31-33 – "So do not worry, saying, 'What shall we eat?' or 'What shall we drink?'... But seek first His kingdom and His righteousness, and all these things will be given to you as well."

How does trusting God's provision free you to live with a thankful heart? What can you thank Him for today that He has faithfully provided?

Action Step: Take a walk outside or spend time in nature today, and thank God for the beauty of creation and His provision for all living things.

_____
_____
_____
_____
_____
_____
_____
_____
_____
_____

Thankfulness and Peace

Isaiah 26:3 – "You will keep in perfect peace those who
minds are steadfast, because they trust in You."

How does thankfulness lead to peace? What situations do you
need to surrender to God to experience His peace?

Action Step: List any burdens weighing on your heart. One by
one, give them to God in prayer and thank Him for His peace.

_____

_____

_____

_____

_____

_____

_____

_____

Thankfulness and Fruit

Galatians 5:22-23 – "But the fruit of the Spirit is love, joy, peace, forbearance, kindness, goodness, faithfulness, gentleness and self-control."

How does thankfulness help you cultivate the fruit of the Spirit? Which fruits can you grow more of in your life through gratitude?

Action Step: Choose one fruit of the Spirit and practice it intentionally today, offering thanks to God for His Spirit at work within you.

Thankfulness for God's Strength

Isaiah 40:31 – "But those who hope in the Lord will ren
their strength. They will soar on wings like eagles; th
will run and not grow weary; they will walk and not
faint. ."

How can thankfulness remind you of God's strength in your
weakness? Where do you need His strength today?

Action Step: When you feel weary today, pause and pray f
strength, then thank God for His power being made perfect in yo
weakness.

Hebrews 13:8 – "Jesus Christ is the same yesterday and today and forever."

How does God's unchanging nature give you peace? In what ways can this truth lead you to gratitude, especially in changing circumstances?

Action Step: Reflect on a change in your life and write down how God's consistent faithfulness has carried you through it.

_____

_____

_____

_____

_____

_____

_____

_____

Gratitude and God's Sovereignty

Romans 8:28 – "And we know that in all things God works for the good of those who love Him, who have been called according to His purpose."

How does knowing God is in control help you live with a heart of thankfulness? What situation do you need to entrust to His sovereignty today?

Action Step: Choose a difficult situation you are facing and thank God for how He will work it for good, even if you can't see it yet.

_____
_____
_____
_____
_____
_____
_____
_____

Psalm 136:1 – "Give thanks to the Lord, for He is good. His love endures forever."

How can you make thankfulness a daily practice in your life? What habits can you put in place to keep gratitude at the forefront?

Action Step: Commit to continuing a daily gratitude practice beyond these 30 days by journaling or praying your thanks to God each morning.

_____

_____

_____

_____

_____

_____

_____

_____

_____

_____

www.ingramcontent.com/pod-product-compliance
Lightning Source LLC
Chambersburg PA
CBHW060241030426
42335CB00014B/1567